DIRECTOR'S MANUAL
FOR WEEKDAY
MINISTRIES

Barbara Snell McLain

DISCIPLESHIP RESOURCES

PO BOX 340003 • NASHVILLE, TN 37203-0003
www.discipleshipresources.org

Cover and book design by Joey McNair

Edited by Debra D. Smith and David Whitworth

ISBN 0-88177-383-2

Library of Congress Control Number: 2002103063

DR383

CONTENTS

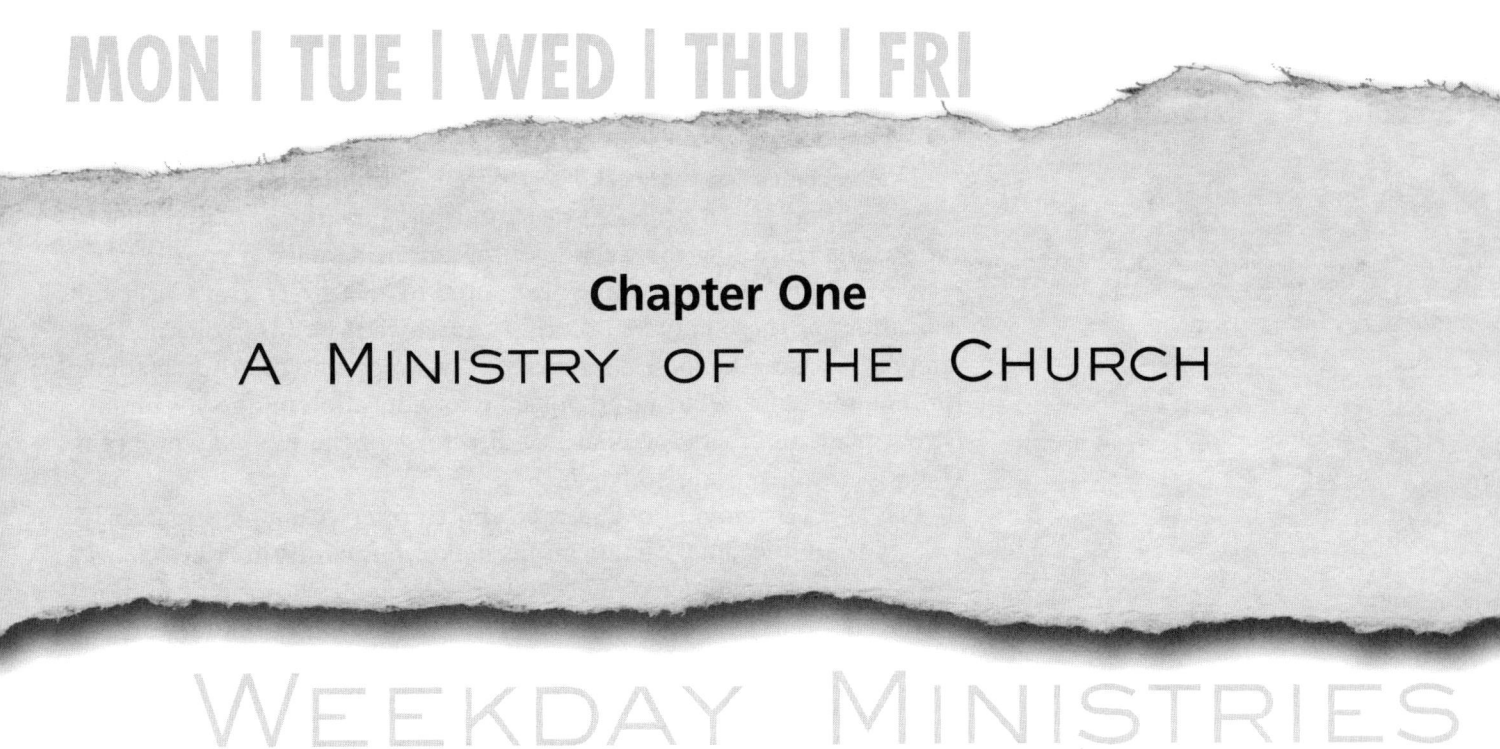

Chapter One
A MINISTRY OF THE CHURCH

WEEKDAY MINISTRIES

The Minister of the Weekday Program

You may never have envisioned yourself as a minister—a Bible in one hand, a list of individual needs in the other, and a prayer always on your lips. As the director of a United Methodist weekday program, you *are* doing ministry. The United Methodist Church proclaims the ministry of all Christians. You may not be called to a ministry of preaching or offering the sacraments, but you have been called to use your gifts to make a difference in the lives of others. In this way, you will discover that you are both a servant and a leader.

Servant leadership comes with both privileges and obligations. It is a privilege to prepare the congregation, and perhaps your community, for the mission of God through childcare and early education. Your obligation is to embody the teachings of Jesus so that those around you, both children and adults, will be better equipped for Christian discipleship.

Your Servant Leadership Role

The ministry of a weekday program director can vary greatly from one setting to the next. The community, the church, and the program focus determine what your responsibilities will include. A large metropolitan church may employ you as a full-time member of the church staff. A small, rural church may hire you to work on a part-time basis. Some settings may require you to speak more than one language in order to fulfill your servant leadership role, while others may require experience working with children who face certain challenges.

Each Situation Is Unique

The placement of the weekday program within the church may also vary. You may be an ordained deacon or the director of Christian education, with directing the weekday program being part of your larger responsibilities. You may have been hired by the director of Christian education, or there may be no other church staff besides you and the appointed pastor. In some churches you will report to the church council through the ministry group responsible for education or age-level ministries, while in others the board of directors for the weekday program serves as the governing body.

Just as each community and each church offers a unique situation, so your gifts and personal qualifications make you unique in your role as a weekday-program director. Who you are determines how you can most effectively fulfill your call to servant leadership. Your education, experience, employment history, and personality all make you who you are. Some program directors have only the educational requirements necessary for state licensing. Others have college degrees in education, perhaps even advanced degrees or endorsements. You may have worked in similar positions for many years, or you may now be facing a new and challenging ministry as weekday-program director for the first time.

Whatever your personal gifts are, they can be useful in your position. As weekday-program director you will need to be a good organizer, yet have the ability to be spontaneous. You will need to be able to meet people easily, yet have a clear understanding of yourself. You will need to be able to gather facts and materials as well as know how to make a competent decision regarding those facts and materials.

What Needs Does the Program Address?

Consider these facts about American children:

1 in 3 is born to unmarried parents.
1 in 3 will be poor at some point in childhood.
1 in 3 is behind a year or more in school.
1 in 5 was born poor.
1 in 5 is born to a mother who did not graduate from high school.
3 in 5 preschoolers have mothers in the labor force.
1 in 6 is born to a mother who did not receive prenatal care in the first three months of pregnancy.
1 in 12 has a disability.
1 in 60 sees their parents divorce in any year.

© Children's Defense Fund. From "The State of America's Children Yearbook 2001: 25 Key Facts About American Children" (www.childrensdefense.org/keyfacts.htm).

These facts reveal the needs of many of America's children. You, as a weekday-ministry director, should be aware of the needs faced by children and their families in your own community. Only then will you be able to structure a program for moving in the direction that it needs to go and to articulate the importance of the program to the church and the community. Established programs should reassess the needs of the community on a regular basis.

A Mother's-Day-Out program that was established in 1982 may no longer be viable if more parents work outside the home on a full-time basis and no longer need short periods of drop-in care. In a neighborhood that offers many full-day childcare options, an afterschool program might meet a greater unmet need for children who are unsupervised after school. Early childhood education through a preschool program would meet a need in an area where children lack opportunities for structured learning. There might be a need for an early childhood education program that teaches Christian values and Bible stories as another option for parents. In every community there are needs that go unmet. Learn to recognize the need and be able to communicate that need to others.

List needs of children in your community.

Why the Church Is an Appropriate Place to Meet Community Needs

The ministry of Jesus Christ was a ministry of meeting needs. Jesus helped people who were sick. He taught those who wanted to know about the mysteries of life by answering questions and telling them stories that helped them deal with the most significant issues in their lives. Jesus helped the blind to see, the deaf to hear, and the lame to rise and walk. He also brought new life into the bodies of some people for whom others mourned, resigned to the fact that they were dead.

The church is here to continue the ministry of Jesus Christ. It is called to be the body of Christ, the embodiment of Christ's love. Today Jesus continues to minister to the world's needs through the people of the church. Where there is a need in the community, the church can act as the eyes, the ears, the hands, and the voice of Jesus Christ.

List the needs your program addresses.

The United Methodist Church has a theological foundation from which ministry to children and their families is most appropriate. The theology of grace as "the undeserved, unmerited, and loving action of God in human existence through the ever-present Holy Spirit" (From *The Book of Discipline of The United Methodist Church—2000*. Copyright © 2000 by The United Methodist Publishing House; ¶ 101, page 45. Used by permission.) is a call to all Christians to reach out to others in ways that will allow them to experience God's love. This may be done through providing a safe place for childcare or by encouraging a child to explore the wonders of God's world. People do not earn God's love by being good enough or knowing the Bible well enough. The theology of grace proclaims that, through Jesus Christ, God loves all people long before they realize it or can understand how God is working in their lives. That is why The United Methodist Church allows infants to be brought by their parents to receive the sacrament of holy baptism. Baptism is a covenant between God, the child's parents, and the congregation. It is an agreement wherein each party makes a promise. Parents promise to bring the child up in a way that will communicate God's love, as witnessed in Jesus Christ, to their son or daughter. The congregation promises to support the child and parents in that endeavor. The water is a symbol of God's grace that is poured over the child. By upholding these promises, the child will grow up knowing himself or herself to be a beloved child of God and will one day publicly profess his or her own faith in God.

List the places where the needs of children in your community intersect with the needs your program addresses.

If you understand the theological base of The United Methodist Church and the needs in your own community, you can determine what type of program will best meet those needs. If your program has been in place for many years, a reassessment of community needs will determine when a change in program structure or content needs to be made.

Developing a Mission: Types of Programs

Programs vary as much as individual communities and churches vary. There are many options. Some options that have been offered as ministries by churches are listed here.

Parent's Day Out

A Parent's-Day-Out program can look different from one church to the next. In one church it may consist of volunteers who sit in the church nursery for a few hours one day a week so that parents can have some free time for themselves. One church operated a Parent's-Day-Out program in coordination with the local WIC (Women, Infants, and Children) program at the health department that was located across the street from the church. This ministry allowed mothers to attend the WIC events without having to worry about their children getting too restless or noisy.

In another church, the Parent's-Day-Out program might consist of paid employees who offer educational experiences for young children once or twice a week. Some churches, however, that refer to their weekday program as "Parent's Day Out" are in actuality offering a preschool or daycare program. Be leery of a church that uses the term *Parent's Day Out* as a way to avoid the state licensing process. Each state defines its terms by the number of hours a week the program operates, the number of children who participate in the program, and the content of the program. Avoid a potentially embarrassing situation by knowing how your state defines the term *Parent's Day Out,* and always abide by your state's minimum licensing requirements. More will be said about licensing in the next chapter.

Are there unmet needs that your weekday program could address?

Preschool

Preschool is usually a half-day program for children ranging from age three to kindergarten eligibility. Preschools have a planned curriculum and might employ paid staff or a combination of paid staff and parents or other volunteers. The focus of a preschool is on developmentally appropriate activities that enrich a child's physical, emotional, social, cognitive, and sometimes spiritual growth.

Daycare Center

A daycare center cares for children from infancy to school age while parents work or attend school. It is open at least nine to ten hours each weekday. A daycare center may have a planned curriculum, but it also provides meals and snacks for the children and includes a nap time.

Emergency or Sick-Child Care

Emergency or sick-child care can be a tremendous ministry for working parents whose child is sick or whose regular daycare provider is sick or on vacation. This kind of program must be in place and easily adaptable, as child participants can vary from day to day. Last-minute notification of the need for care is normal for this type of program. Particular attention needs to be paid to the dispensing of prescription and over-the-counter medications to sick children. It can be helpful to have a nurse on staff or to establish a relationship with a consulting physician. Parent communication throughout the day is essential for this type of childcare.

Special-Needs Care

Family with children who have special needs can often have a difficult time finding reliable childcare. Children with extra physical, mental, or emotional needs can benefit from a ministry designed specifically for them. This type of program requires careful planning and a staff with training in the area of special needs.

Before- and Afterschool Programs

Childcare programs for infants and preschoolers are numerous in many areas. However, care for school-aged children whose parents work outside the home before school starts or after school is out can be a concern for many families. Before- and afterschool programs provide a safe place for children and may include a snack, recreational activities, and sometimes homework time or tutoring. A church program may include a Christian education component.

Deciding which type of program will best meet the particular needs in your community can determine whether your weekday program will flourish, die out, or never get off the ground.

Ministry in a Connectional System

Since your ministry will be lived out within the walls of a United Methodist church, it is essential that you understand the structure of the church and how to work within that structure.

The United Methodist Church is part of a connectional system. No individual church is governed solely on its own; all are part of a larger network. The denomination is made up of local churches, districts, and annual conferences that are all part of the General Conference. If you are not familiar with this structure, talk to your pastor about materials that will help you get acquainted with it. At each level—local church, district, conference, and General Conference—there are resources that will be beneficial to you and the weekday ministry you direct.

The Book of Discipline of The United Methodist Church is the document in which the theological statement, the Social Principles, and the structure and governance of the denomination are printed. *The Book of Discipline* is updated every four years by the General Conference. At that time, lay and clergy delegates from each annual conference gather to celebrate and discern God's direction in matters concerning the structure, the doctrine, and the social stances of The United Methodist Church.

What type of program do you direct?

What other types of programs are available in your community?

For a detailed description of how The United Methodist Church is organized, read pages 153 to 169 of *The Book of Discipline of The United Methodist Church—2000*. If your church library does not have a copy, ask to borrow one from your pastor.

The Local Church Structure

Within each local church there is a church council that is responsible for planning and implementing the nurture, outreach, and witness ministries of the congregation. How the church council is structured and organized may differ from church to church, often depending on the size of the church membership. You will need to be familiar with the church council and the ministry groups that report to this decision-making body. January is when most church officers and committee members begin new terms, with a three-year term being fairly typical. Some of the individuals and groups that a weekday-ministry director works most closely with are mentioned here.

The Pastor

The pastor is the person appointed to serve the church by preaching the word, offering the sacraments, and overseeing the administration of the church. The pastor is usually an ordained elder or a local pastor. A good working relationship with the pastor is essential. Since many pastors do not have a background in childhood education, it is your responsibility to inform him or her of the importance of the weekday ministry and how it enhances the ministry of the entire church. When a new pastor is appointed to the church, introduce her or him to the weekday ministry. Invite the pastor to visit the program. Help the pastor to see how the weekday ministry is part of the pulse of the church and not just an added attraction.

The Church Office Staff

The church office staff may consist of one part-time secretary or many people serving many roles in the church office. There may be an office manager, an administrator of finance, a secretary, and so forth. All of these people are part of the support system for the weekday ministry. The church secretary often handles the church calendar. Check with the secretary when scheduling anything or planning to use space outside of the designated program room. This will save a lot of last-minute hassles as well as hurt feelings over misunderstandings and missed communication links. In some churches, the church finance administrator handles the weekday ministry's financial records. She or he may write the checks for the program, pay the program staff, and audit the books annually. This, of course, depends on how the program has been set up.

Director of Christian Education

Some churches employ a director of Christian education (DCE). Often, this person is an ordained deacon or diaconal minister who oversees the educational ministries of the church. Sometimes the DCE is the weekday-ministry director. Often the weekday-program director is accountable to the DCE. A good working relationship between the DCE and the program director is a must if the program is going to be successful.

Ministry Group Responsible for Education

In most churches there will be a ministry group or groups responsible for the educational ministries of the church. This group may be called the nurture ministry group, the education committee, the work area on education, the educational ministries team, or some other name unique to your congregation. Some congregations will have a group that focuses on educational ministries specifically with children, often referred to as a children's council or something similar.

Whatever the group is called, often the weekday-ministry program is related to this ministry area. In some churches the director of the weekday program serves as a member of this group. In other churches the chairperson of the board of directors of the weekday ministry acts as a liaison between this group and the weekday program. Again, each church and each program can be structured differently. As the director of a weekday program it is very important that you have a clear understanding of how the weekday program relates both programmatically and administratively to the whole church.

Sunday School Superintendent and Teachers

If you are using space that is also used for Sunday school, it is important that you work closely with the Sunday school superintendent and the teachers who use that space on Sunday mornings. Many problems can be avoided if there is open and honest communication between the weekday-ministry director and the Sunday school department. Work together to come up with solutions to issues before they become a major concern.

Board of Trustees

The board of trustees oversees the upkeep of the church facilities. This is the group you would go to if you wanted to paint the walls or set up a playgroup area outside. It is always helpful to give an annual report to the board of trustees as well as an annual tour through the weekday-ministry space.

Church Custodian

The church custodian is another person who needs to be consulted in order to work out potential problem areas. Who cleans the bathroom used by the weekday ministry? What is expected of the program director and teachers as far as cleaning up the room, and what is expected of the church custodian?

United Methodist Women

United Methodist Women (UMW) is often one of the most active groups in the church. They frequently have a particular interest in and commitment to ministries that affect children. A weekday ministry may find many resources within the UMW, volunteers as well as possible monetary support or assistance with fundraising projects.

The Kitchen Committee

Many churches have a committee that is responsible for overseeing the use of the church kitchen. In large churches there may be a staff person who manages the kitchen. Be sure you communicate with this group or with the individual who takes care of kitchen matters. This committee needs to know when and how the weekday ministry will be using the church kitchen. The weekday program needs to know the policies and procedures involved in use of the church kitchen.

List the people who fill these positions, their phone numbers, and any other needed contact information.

Pastor

Director of Christian Education

Secretary

Financial Administrator

Custodian

Chair of Educational Ministries

Sunday School Superintendent

Chair of Trustees

UMW President

Kitchen Coordinator

All of these groups and individuals are important for maintaining a successful weekday ministry. Remember, you are part of a team called the church. Having been chosen to serve as program director because of the knowledge and gifts you bring, and having a clear understanding of the needs the program addresses, you and the rest of the church can work together to develop a ministry that will touch the lives of many as you live out your servant leadership role.

Chapter Two
OFFERING A QUALITY PROGRAM

WEEKDAY MINISTRIES

Characteristics of a Quality Program

The quality of a weekday program will determine its failure or success. Quality is reflected in three areas: the safety of the environment, developmentally appropriate content, and the expression of values that are unique to your situation.

A Safe Environment

A safe environment ensures that both children and their parents will feel comfortable about the surroundings. A safe environment requires an awareness of potential hazards in the space where the program takes place. This includes everything from electrical outlet plugs to the emotional stability of the adults who are present in and around the program. Safety is a priority for state licensing of a program, and licensing packets will help evaluate the safety of your environment.

Developmentally Appropriate Practices

Developmentally appropriate practices have to do with designing the content of a program in such a way that children can naturally relate to it. Children must relate to the content through their interests, needs, and competencies. As age is only one factor in determining what is appropriate, the National Association for the Education of Young Children (an organization discussed at the end of the chapter) points out that developmentally appropriate practice takes into account other elements as well. Developmentally appropriate practice has to do with designing all aspects of a program with these things in mind: an understanding of how children develop and learn, knowledge of individual children in the program, and an awareness of the social and cultural environment of each child.

Safety check

- Is the hot water heater turned down to ensure that children cannot burn themselves?

- Are all poisonous items kept out of reach and locked up?

- Is refrigeration available and reliable for food items?

- Are the heating and air conditioning appropriate for the comfort of children and adults?

- Are toys kept clean and sanitary?

- Are restroom facilities easily accessible?

List other safety issues for your program.

Five-year-olds can master some skills that are beyond the ability of most three-year-olds. Because some children do not have a male role model in the home, it may not be appropriate to assume that all children understand the concept of "daddy" as a member of the family. If a child comes from a Spanish-speaking home, a program that is taught exclusively in English would not be appropriate. All of these aspects contribute to the quality of a developmentally appropriate program.

Unique Values

The values that are unique to your situation contribute to the quality of the program. The fact that the program is a ministry of the church makes it different from one offered by a for-profit chain or by a secular not-for-profit organization. The program will reflect the theological and social values of The United Methodist Church. Acceptance of all people is a practice that reflects the teachings of Christ. The way in which you act out this practice will, of course, depend on the accessibility of your space and the training of staff. Your program may not be equipped to meet the needs of a child who is severely disabled, but you can be prepared to make a caring referral to that child's family. You may choose to accept all people, with the understanding that they are aware that the content will reflect biblical teachings. Or you may offer a ministry to "all God's children," regardless of faith background. Both are legitimate ministries of the church. A program designed to teach Bible stories as part of the content will be different from any program offered through public organizations. Discernment through prayer as to how God calls the church to care for children is a vital and ongoing necessity for a quality program.

The Local Resource and Referral Agency

Of value to any program is the local resource and referral agency that serves your area. This agency will have a list of programs in your area. Such a list can be helpful in establishing a cooperative relationship with other programs, in knowing what is available for children with special needs, and possibly even in developing a support network in your own area. The local resource and referral agency can give you information on licensing and offers workshops for continuing education and training that is required in most places. Sometimes the resource and referral agency provides activity boxes and program ideas that have been suggested by the various programs in the area.

To get in touch with the agency in your area, contact your licensing agency or ask another program director in your area. They are usually happy to assist you. The resource and referral agency can answer many questions you have as you start and maintain a quality program. They are aware of your state requirements and the needs in the area. You can also find out about your local resource and referral agency by contacting the National Association of Child Care Resource and Referral Agencies (NACCRRA), 1319 F. Street NW, Suite 500, Washington, DC 20004; 202-393-5501; www.naccrra.org.

Licensing

A quality program is a program that is licensed by the state. The purpose of licensing is to ensure a safe, healthy, quality program. Even if your state offers exemption from licensing to religious organizations, it is in the best interest of the children and the program providers to pursue licensing. Licensing is based on meeting the minimum standards required by the state. The church needs to seek at least the minimum requirements, and hopefully exceed them. This should be done willingly and with a focus on ministry, rather than grudgingly. Beware programs that choose to avoid licensing because they are religious programs. Licensing reflects a concern and care for the children involved.

Since there are no national childcare regulations, each state differs in requirements. Contact your state licensure body in the early stages of envisioning a weekday ministry so that these requirements will be included in each stage of planning.

The Licensing Packet

The licensing packet gives you your instructions and workbook for the licensing procedure. Do not be overwhelmed by the size of it all. The packet is something that the board of directors or program planning committee can work through together. Use it as a tool to bring people on board. The church trustees will need to be aware of space and equipment requirements as well as fire-safety requirements. Some of the requirements that are included in the licensing packet are as follows.

Licensing Capacity

Licensing capacity is usually determined by available space and the credentials and number of staff. A small program would minister to 12 or fewer children, while a large program might minister to more than 160 children. If you are just starting a program, it is wise to start small.

Fire Safety

State fire-safety requirements must be met for licensing. For many churches this can lead to major expenses related to the building. A church that has never installed smoke detectors or fire alarms can be looking at thousands of dollars for installation. Yet this is not an issue solely for the weekday ministry; it is an issue of safety for the entire congregation. Some states require that facilities have interconnecting smoke detectors. Others need an alarm system. Every facility is required to have a fire-escape plan that is posted in each room and to practice a monthly fire drill. Fire safety is an issue that churches need to take seriously. A place where candles burn regularly and people are in and out all week long is a dangerous place to be if fire safety is not being practiced. You might present the problem to the administrative council or to the board of trustees by stating, "In the process of making plans for a weekday ministry, it has been brought to our attention that our church does not presently meet minimum fire-safety requirements." Draw on the expertise of the local fire department or an individual in the church who may be employed by the fire department.

What are some specific uniquenesses that your church and situation have to offer through your weekday ministry?

List the location and phone number of the resource and referral agency nearest you.

15

Health Inspection

Typically, a facility is inspected annually by the county or state as a requirement for licensure. The inspector looks at health and safety issues related to floors and carpeting, windows and doors, lighting, food preparation, toileting and diapering, and more. Think of the inspection as a tool for making your program a healthy one for those involved.

Zoning Approval

Before operating a childcare or education program, be sure that the program fits the zoning laws in your area. This is usually not a problem for programs that are housed within the church building. But if, for example, the church will be using a house in the next block as the site for the weekday ministry, zoning laws must be taken into account in order to meet licensing regulations.

Space Requirements

States differ in the amount of space required for each child in the program. In Texas, for example, there must be at least 30 square feet of indoor space for each child. This does not include restrooms and kitchens that are used for a single use. In Kansas, the required floor space per child is 35 feet.

Outdoor space requirements differ as well. Eighty square feet of outdoor play space is required for each child in Texas, while Kansas requires at least 75 square feet.

Furnishings and Equipment

Typically, programs are required to provide chairs and tables that are a comfortable size for the children in the program and in good repair so as not to cause safety concerns. A working telephone must be present. Restrooms need to be available and accessible to the children. Sinks and refrigeration are necessary if food is to be stored or prepared. Be cautious of restroom doors that have locks on the inside when offering a program for children under six years of age. These kind of issues will be addressed in detail in the licensing packet.

Disciplinary Policy

The packet will outline what an appropriate disciplinary policy includes and does not include. The methods you choose to incorporate into the disciplinary policy need to be written up, printed in your handbooks, and posted in the program facilities.

Emergency Procedures

Fire drills are one emergency procedure. Along with a fire-escape plan, there will need to be a plan that can easily be set into action in the case of sudden illness or injury. In most parts of the country, a procedure for tornadoes or other severe weather is required to be posted and practiced.

Animals and Pets

The licensing packet will set forth regulations regarding any animals that are on the premises or any pets that are kept at the program site. Vaccination and care issues will be addressed.

Records to Keep

Records are a way of keeping important information easily accessible. This includes staff records, records for the children, and facility records.

Staff records to be kept on file might include
1. Name, date of birth, address, telephone number, and copies of two forms of identification;
2. Education, training and experience, and continuing education documentation;
3. Health record, including current health card and/or physician's statement verifying the employee is free of contagious tuberculosis;
4. Employment record and documentation of contact made or attempted with former employers;
5. Review of alcohol and drug abuse policy and procedure;
6. Attendance record, listing days and hours worked;
7. Date of employment and date of separation;
8. Authorization for release of confidential information contained in the state Child Abuse and Neglect Central Registry;
9. Request for criminal record check;
10. Employee-performance evaluation tools;
11. Completed Employee's Withholding Allowance Certificate (W-4);
12. Completed Employment Eligibility Verification form (I-9).

Records for children would include
1. Attendance;
2. Physical form that is signed by a physician or health nurse and includes a record of up-to-date immunizations;
3. Form tracking the child's physical and social development;
4. Parental permissions for field trips;
5. Emergency phone numbers, hospital preference, and a list of people who are authorized to pick the child up from the program;
6. Documentation of any illnesses, accidents, bruises, or behavior patterns.

Facility records document things such as
1. Fire drills;
2. Tornado drills;
3. Fire-safety inspection;
4. Annual health inspection;
5. Fire-extinguisher check;
6. Accident reports;
7. Contagious illnesses among program participants;
8. Tuition records;
9. Financial records;
10. Facility and equipment repairs and needs.

Transportation and Field Trips

The licensing packet will also outline requirements necessary for the transportation of children and for field trips. A vehicle-safety checklist and state regulations on child safety seats are likely to be included.

What children's records are appropriate for your program?

What facility records are appropriate for your program?

Accreditation

Accreditation through a nationally recognized organization is one way to ensure the quality of the program. Accreditation requires more than the minimum state licensing requirements. Organizations such as the National Association for the Education of Young Children (NAEYC), the Ecumenical Child Care Network (ECCN), and the National School-Age Care Alliance (NSACA) can lead you through an accreditation process that can help evaluate an existing ministry and make quality improvements. Accreditation is often viewed as a higher stamp of approval by those seeking quality programs for their children. (Contact information for all three organizations can be found in Chapter 14.)

The National Association for the Education of Young Children (NAEYC)

The National Association for the Education of Young Children is the most influential organization in the U.S. of early childhood educators and others who seek quality programs for children from birth through third grade. Whether your weekday ministry consists of a daycare center, preschool, or before- and afterschool childcare, it could benefit by a connection with the NAEYC.

NAEYC accreditation comes through the National Academy of Early Childhood Programs and is based on the Academy's Criteria for High Quality Early Childhood Programs.

The process is voluntary and threefold. There is a self-study, followed by validation, and then the accreditation decision. There are fees for the first two steps, which is why many programs choose not to seek accreditation. For more information, contact the Academy.

The Ecumenical Child Care Network (ECCN)

A professional association of early childhood educators, the ECCN addresses the issues of church-based programs. Membership in ECCN will allow you access to the ECCN newsletter, publications, and the National Council on Recognition (NCR), which offers a self-study to church-based childcare programs. Many of the publications put out by ECCN contain practical and helpful information for church-based childcare programs.

National School-Age Care Alliance (NSACA)

NSACA is a nationwide organization that represents public, private, and community-based providers of afterschool programs for children and youth, ages five to fourteen. Quality school-age care is the mission of NSACA. Detailed standards have been developed to help school-age programs meet this high quality of care. NSACA offers a three-step accreditation and program-improvement system known as the Advancing and Recognizing Quality (ARQ) system. The first step is to purchase the NSACA Standards of Quality School-Age Care to be used as a tool to help identify needed improvements. Step two is to purchase and complete the Self-Study and Accreditation Kit. Step three is to apply for accreditation, which will come after an endorsement visit by NSACA. More information can be obtained by contacting NSACA.

In making choices about licensing, memberships, and accreditation, keep in mind that the purpose is to provide the best quality of care through which children and their families will experience the love of Jesus Christ. Requirements that take the most time, energy, money, or commitment often prove to be the most valuable services a church leader can offer the people of God.

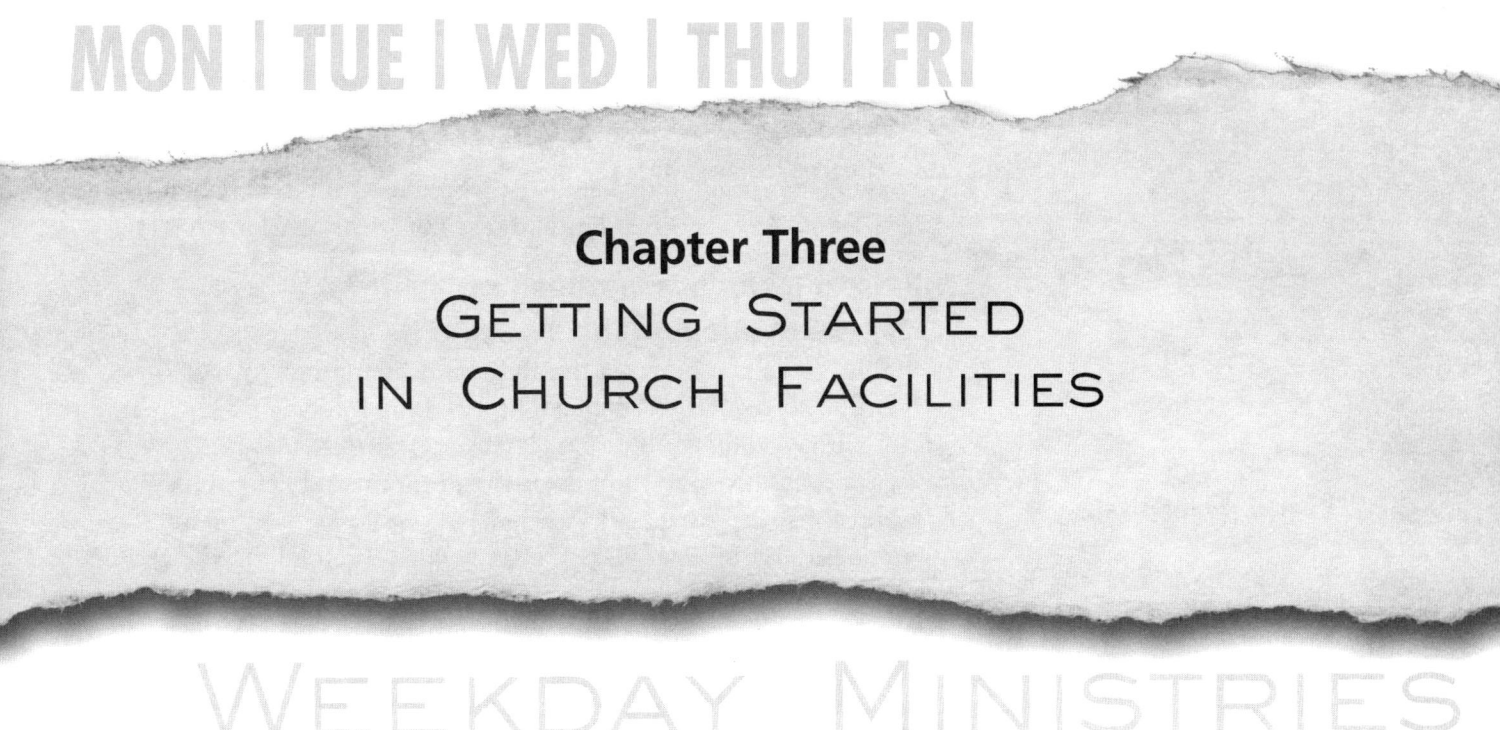

Chapter Three
GETTING STARTED IN CHURCH FACILITIES

WEEKDAY MINISTRIES

The Church and the Weekday Program in Covenant

The church as a whole and any group or organization that functions either as part of the church or within the church building need to establish a relationship that is conducive to the ministry of Jesus Christ. Just like a family, in which all members lead individual lives yet still affect one another's lives, the church and the weekday program must exist in covenant relationship.

A covenant is an agreement between two parties, each having certain privileges and responsibilities. The church has privileges as the organization that makes the weekday ministry possible, but it also takes on new responsibilities with each ministry that takes place in the name of that church. The weekday-ministry program likewise has privileges associated with its place in the church, but it too has responsibilities associated with the church's total ministry and with using church facilities to house its activity.

An Independently Run, Church-Housed Program

When the weekday ministry is run by someone outside of the local church who is merely using space provided by the church, a covenant relationship is vital. Whether the program is church-sponsored or not, if it takes place within the walls of the church and uses the name of the church to identify its location, that program will be associated with the church in the minds of people in the community. The church, therefore, has a responsibility to communicate its expectations to the program. Issues related to upkeep and maintenance of the facility, practices that may reflect ideologies contrary to those held by the church, building and supply expenses, and rights to space all need to be addressed. A written covenant ensures that all parties are presented with the same words and serves as a concrete representation of the covenant relationship.

Things to Include in a Covenant With an Outside Organization

- Establish a liaison between the church and the program.
- Determine a regularly scheduled time for the leaders of the program to meet with the liaison to discuss issues and concerns.
- List expenses involved in housing the program and determine who is responsible for paying each expense.
- Decide if the program will pay a set "expense refund" to the church. Be careful about asking for "rent" as a non-profit organization. Renting to a for-profit organization may endanger the church's tax status. Check with your annual conference finance and administration chair.
- Decide who will be responsible for routine cleaning of the area used by the program.
- Decide who will be responsible for seasonal cleaning of the area used by the program.
- Require that the church have a copy of the liability insurance policy held by the program.
- Prepare a church calendar for the program leaders and ask for a program calendar from them.
- Designate off-limit space, time, supplies, and equipment.
- Outline expectations of program staff while in the church building.
- Set up a time schedule for review of the agreement to house the program and a date at which the agreement can be terminated by the church. A yearly assessment is a good idea.
- Determine the process by which property damage will be handled.
- Decide who will be granted licenses and permits.

Make the written covenant as clear and concise as possible and always consult an attorney who is familiar with church law and polity when drawing up the covenant.

When the Program Is a Ministry of the Church

When the weekday program is a ministry of the church, many of the same issues will apply. Regular communications can be set up through the existing structure of the local church. Again, a written covenant is helpful as a concrete tool for understanding the responsibilities and privileges of the parties involved. In many cases, the weekday ministry is a ministry of the church with, however, a separate administrative and financial structure. The process of writing up a covenant can help churches come to an understanding of the expectations and responsibilities of all involved and perhaps iron out some of the wrinkles before they become problems. The church is made up of individual people with unique personalities and roles within the church. Communication and understanding among all the people involved is an essential element for the success of any ministry. A written covenant can be a place to begin this ongoing process.

The People of the Covenant

The Pastor

The role of the pastor in the weekday ministry will vary from church to church. In a church where the weekday ministry is the brainchild of the pastor, she or he can be expected to be quite involved in all aspects of the development of the program. In other situations the pastor will be thrilled to have someone else spearhead the plans and administer the details of a weekday ministry. You are likely to be that person. Regardless of the situation, the pastor remains the one appointed to the church for the purpose of overseeing the order of the church. Clear and regular communication with the pastor about the weekday ministry is essential.

Office Staff

The time and availability of church staff to the weekday ministry may need to be negotiated. Is the church secretary responsible for running off copies of letters or activity sheets for the weekday ministry? Who types up the program handbooks? Is the church financial secretary responsible for keeping records for the weekday ministry as well? Guidelines for use of the copy machine, the church computer, and the secretary's time need to be understood by the weekday-ministry staff as well as the church staff.

Board of Trustees

As overseers of the church property, the board of trustees will need to work with the weekday ministry with regard to the upkeep of the facility. Someone needs to be designated as the person who can be called upon in the event that repairs must be made. The board of trustees is the group you will need to work with if you desire to construct an outdoor playground or add a child-sized toilet. Any building or property concerns are the work of the board of trustees.

Staff-Parish Relations Committee

This is the group in the church to whom the church staff is accountable. The director of the weekday ministry may also be accountable to the staff-parish relations committee. In some churches, the program director is accountable to the Christian education director, who is in turn accountable to the committee. In other churches, the program director is accountable to the board of directors of the weekday ministry. The chairperson of the board of directors reports to the church council or the group designated by the church council. However the lines of accountability are worked out in your church, they need to be drawn out clearly so that everyone knows to whom they should report.

Church Custodian

The church custodian can be a tremendous support to the weekday ministry or can make things quite difficult. Working with the custodian to understand who is responsible for cleaning the space used by the weekday program is essential. Who cleans the restrooms? Who sweeps the classroom floor? Who keeps paper towels well-supplied in the child-care center? These details need to be worked out so that no one feels as though he or she is being taken advantage of or being ignored.

If there is a director of Christian education, other than yourself, on staff at your church, that person can be a valuable resource for you and the weekday ministry. Use the training and experience that the DCE has to enhance the weekday ministry.

Kitchen Committee

The kitchen committee is often a person or group of people designated by United Methodist Women. If you will be using the kitchen for the weekday program, you will need the support of the kitchen committee. To make things as easy as possible, it is a good idea to draw up guidelines for the use of the kitchen. These may already be in place. Go over the guidelines with the kitchen committee, making sure that you understand their expectations and that they understand your program needs. If you will be using utensils or drinking glasses that are exclusively meant for the weekday ministry, they will need to be labeled, and a space will need to be designated for their storage. Refrigerator items should also be labeled so another group does not assume that the tray of cookies in there is meant for them. Possible conflicts with the use of the kitchen should be addressed before they occur. For example, how is the kitchen used when a funeral dinner or a district or conference event is to take place in the church? Work out as many of these things as possible before they come up.

Sunday School Teachers Who Share the Space

When the weekday ministry takes place in a room that is also used for Sunday school, the Sunday school teacher and director of the weekday ministry will need to work together cooperatively. Together they will need to determine what equipment and supplies will be shared and what will be separate. They will then need to decide who is to pay for any shared supplies. Anything that is to be kept separate should be stored in labeled storage areas. A Sunday school teacher may need to give up some storage space for supplies used by the weekday ministry.

All of these people, as well as the rest of the congregation, are part of the covenant made between a church and a weekday ministry. Open and regular communication between the people of the covenant is the best tool to ensure positive relations and a feeling of support among those involved. Plan regular meeting times with these people in order to ask questions and iron out problems before they get out of control.

Collecting Equipment and Supplies

When just beginning a weekday ministry, the list of needed equipment and supplies can seem overwhelming. But when you stop to think about it, you may already have many of these things. Other items can be donated, made by somebody in the church or community, or purchased for a reasonable price at a garage sale.

Necessary equipment may include child-sized tables and chairs, storage bins for each child to store his or her belongings, developmentally appropriate toys and puzzles, outdoor equipment that meets safety regulations, resting mats or cots, and so on. Take time to list every piece of equipment you think you may need, from diaper pails to outdoor climbers.

Having made the list, put a check mark next to all equipment which either you or the church can already provide. Small chairs may already be available as well as some of the toys in the church nursery. Then, write the letter D next to anything that someone might be willing to donate.

Maybe some of the people in the church would be willing to donate toys. Place the letter B next to any equipment that you or someone you know might be able to build. A balance beam can be made quite easily and inexpensively, for example. Next, write a P next to those items you will have to purchase. You will need to decide who will pay for these items and who has the privilege of using them. If you buy a paint easel for the weekday ministry, will it be accessible equipment for the Sunday school teacher? Deciding this at or before the time of purchase will spare you from many problems in the future.

The same kind of activity can be done for supplies such as construction paper, paintbrushes, paint, crayons, scissors, collage materials, and so forth. List every supply you will need to begin. Mark off those that are already available. Determine which supplies can be donated or made or need to be purchased. Who is to pay for them and who has the privilege of using them?

Including the Congregation Along the Way

It is important that the weekday ministry be a ministry of the entire church and not just of an individual or a small group within the church. The congregation needs to be kept on board as plans are being made and as the ministry unfolds. Keep the congregation informed through church newsletter reports, Sunday morning announcements, and bulletin board displays. Invite people from the congregation to participate in the weekday ministry. Some will be willing to build equipment or to put together some supplies. Others will be able to help prepare the space used by the program. Still others will have skills and talents that can be used some way in the weekday ministry. Invite as many people from the congregation as you can to participate in as many ways as you can think of.

Celebrate every step along the way with the congregation. You may want to consider some of the following vehicles for celebration: a kick-off ice-cream social; milestone recognitions; open houses; a commissioning of the board of directors; weekday-ministry project displays; a formal list of donors and contributors published in the church newsletter; endless thanks. This will help people feel a sense of ownership and pride in the ministry that takes place during the week.

Every member of the church should be invited to pray for the weekday ministry. Prayers can be incorporated into the Sunday worship services. Prayers for program staff, the children in the program, and the families who are served by the program can all be offered to God, and every person in the church can participate.

What ways do you currently use to keep the congregation informed about weekday ministries?

What new ways could you try to inform the congregation about weekday ministries?

WEEKDAY MINISTRIES

Chapter Four
STRUCTURING THE WEEKDAY MINISTRY

The Purpose of the Program

The structure of the weekday ministry will be determined by these elements: (1) who the program serves; (2) when they are served; (3) what they will be offered. The question of who the ministry is to serve is the first question that will need to be addressed in the planning stage of a new weekday ministry and in the assessment stage of an existing program. The answer may not be as simple as it first appears. A church that decides to offer a daycare program needs to decide who they will serve. "Children" is too broad an answer. What children? Whose children? What age of children? The rest of the structure cannot develop until these questions are answered.

Who Will You Serve?

Who you will serve will depend on the goals of the ministry. Will you serve the children of church members, neighborhood children, or children throughout the area? The answer to this question will be reflected in the content of the weekday ministry. Choosing to offer a ministry to the children of church members will allow for Christian education to be an integral part of the content. A program offered to "all God's children" may mean living out the love of Christ while not including Bible stories or "God talk" in the content of the curriculum. These guidelines will need to be made clear to everyone involved: church, board of directors, community.

A program that serves the children of Christian families can be marketed as a "Christian Daycare" or as a preschool in which "Christian curriculum" is used. The advantage of this is that the weekday program becomes an evangelism tool in which children and their families are introduced to Bible stories, Christian values, and theological talk at a level that is developmentally appropriate. Theological talk can be as simple as a daily reminder that "God loves you," or as complicated as helping an afterschool group come to a better understanding of the sacraments.

A program that serves children of all faiths and backgrounds is also a valid ministry. In such a program, children experience Christ's love through the care of the staff and learn to appreciate the wonders of the world around them. All of this can happen without Christian labels attached. That the weekday ministry serves all children will need to be clearly understood in the minds of the staff, the congregation, and the families it serves. It will need to be decided how Christmas and Easter will be celebrated. If the birth of Christ will be a focus at Christmas time, that will need to be made clear so that families who feel uncomfortable will have the opportunity to make a choice about allowing their children to participate in the program.

The parent handbook (described later, in Chapter 8) should state clearly the religious content of the program. Here are some examples of handbook statements:

Christian values will be demonstrated at Rainbow Preschool. These include the following messages: "God loves us. We can love God. We can love others. God is always with us. We can trust God. God's world is good. Jesus taught us about God's love." At Christmas we celebrate Jesus' birth. At Easter Jesus shows us that things become new again. Thanksgiving is a time to thank God for everything.

Hobby Horse Daycare is a ministry of the Hope United Methodist Church. We seek to offer care to all of God's children regardless of race, religion, or national origin. Therefore, there will be no religious content incorporated into the daycare program, although staff will demonstrate God's love through their care for the children.

Madison Street United Methodist Church invites all children to participate in the Children's Activity Program (CAP). Although religious education is not a standard part of the CAP curriculum, we will offer Christian education as a club option and will celebrate the birth of Jesus at Christmas. If this teaching is contrary to your belief system, feel free to remove your child from CAP during the two weeks before Christmas and to select other club options.

Whether Christian education is part of the curriculum of the weekday program or not, the program is still a valid ministry as people are cared for by loving staff. The needs of the community will determine the religious content of the program. In a church where there are families who long for an early introduction to Christian education, a Christian-based curriculum would meet a preschool need. In an urban neighborhood where children of all faiths and some of no faith at all would go unsupervised after school, a program that provides a place to go and some structured activities would certainly be a ministry worth extending.

When Will You Serve Them?

The purpose of the program will also determine the time frame in which the weekday ministry will be offered. A daycare program will need to be set up during parents' working hours. This may be from 6:30 A.M. to 6:30 P.M., or it may be designed around the hours of various shifts. A preschool that is separate from daycare will probably be a half-day program. "Half-day" can mean anything from two hours, two days a week to three hours, five days a week. Weekly hours and a yearly calendar need to be set up and posted.

Program hours can be set with the following in mind: needs of the children and their families, availability of staff, availability of space, and the public school schedule.

You may choose to design a ministry in which the hours are what makes it unique. Perhaps there is a need for nighttime childcare in your area. In that case, program hours might be from 6:00 P.M. to 7:00 A.M. Weekend care is another possibility. Remember, the needs of the community and the resources available in the church are the keys to establishing the structure of the weekday ministry.

What Will You Offer Them?

The answer to this question will become the curriculum for the weekday ministry. You will need to know what the purpose and the goals of the program will be in order to design a curriculum that will serve that purpose and meet those goals. Some possible goals are as follows:

To Provide Safe Care

Simply housing a program within a church building does not guarantee safety for children. The safety of a program will depend on staff training; the church's awareness of and guidelines for issues related to the risk of child abuse in the church; environmental health and safety issues; disaster plans and practice; and parents' responsibility in labeling children's belongings, in communicating with the staff about illnesses and absences, and in keeping children home when they are sick.

A staff trained in first aid, in CPR, and in recognizing the signs of child abuse will provide a safety foundation, but safety involves much more. The staff should also be trained in positive discipline void of physical punishment, humiliating consequences for children, or harmful restraints and be expected to uphold a positive discipline policy as determined by the board of directors. There should be a posted plan for fire and storm procedures with drills held monthly. The environment should be free from dangerous objects, harmful chemicals, bugs, rodents, and other unsanitary conditions.

For children to be safe within the walls of the church, the church as a whole will need to put into place a policy and procedure designed to reduce the risk of child abuse. Appropriate background checks need to be made on everyone who will be working around the children. That includes both clergy and laypeople, professionals and volunteers. It is strongly suggested that any church considering a weekday ministry purchase a copy of *Safe Sanctuaries* by Joy Thornburg Melton (Discipleship Resources, 1998) and use it as a resource for discussing and implementing a plan to prevent child abuse.

Child safety also depends on parents. Parents may need to be educated about when it is or is not appropriate to send a child to daycare.

When does your program operate?

What do you offer the children in your program?

Does your church have policies and procedures in place to reduce the risk of child abuse?

Guidelines can be printed in the parent handbook and should be practiced as they are stated. When children come to the weekday ministry with fevers, upset stomachs, or a rash, they are endangering the safety of everyone in the program.

To Provide a Christian Atmosphere

A Christian atmosphere is an environment in which a child experiences, first-hand, Christ-like love and acceptance. Whether the curriculum is explicitly Christian or not, all children can be treated with respect, accepted for who they are, and loved unconditionally. There are times when a child needs a lap to sit in, a high-five for encouragement, an adult who is willing to listen, or the safety of limits. Through all of these things, the love of Christ lives and touches the lives of children.

To Help Children Develop

Healthy child development is an important goal for any program with children. Children grow socially as they interact with other children and are guided by adults who demonstrate cooperative relations with others. Emotional development takes place as children mature in their self-understanding and in their understanding of their own feelings and the feelings of others. Learning appropriate ways to express feelings is an important part of any early childhood program. Cognitive development takes place as children are exposed to activities that encourage problem-solving, memorization, listening skills, and visual discrimination. Children grow spiritually as they learn to trust, love, share, and understand that they are loved. Bible stories and simple statements like "God made you and loves you" can offer a faith foundation that children can build on the rest of their lives. Physical development comes as children are given opportunities to practice motor skills. Fine motor skills are used in writing, cutting with scissors, building with interlocking blocks, and fitting puzzle pieces into place. Gross motor skills develop through running, jumping, climbing, and crawling. All of these developmental areas are enhanced by a clean environment and a healthy diet.

The Purpose Statement

The purpose statement is a brief but clear statement which determines everything else about the program. A purpose statement can be designed by following the outline above: A. Who will you serve? B. When will you serve them? C. What will you offer them? A purpose statement may look something like these:

The purpose of Rainbow Preschool is to provide a Christian atmosphere in which children ages three through five can develop spiritually, socially, emotionally, cognitively, and physically in preparation to enter kindergarten.

The Hobby Horse Daycare Center is a ministry of Hope United Methodist Church to families in the community who need trusted care for children ages six weeks to six years. The program is designed to care for children in a way that will offer them safety, nutrition, and developmentally appropriate experiences throughout the day while their parents are at work.

The Children's Activity Program (CAP) at Madison Street United Methodist Church offers activities for students from Madison Elementary School from 3:30 P.M. to 5:30 P.M. Activities will provide academic assistance when needed, sportsmanship, fun, nutritious snacks, and fellowship with other children in a supervised environment.

What is the purpose statement of your program?

The Curriculum

The curriculum is the "how" of the program. It is the purpose in action. In order to act out the purpose, you need to set goals. Then, in order to meet the goals, you can use objectives as a measuring tool. All of these elements make up the curriculum and ultimately fulfill the purpose of the weekday ministry.

Goals and Objectives

How will the purpose of the program be fulfilled? Through the goals that are set, the purpose will be realized. Goals should be specific, with enough flexibility to allow for developmental differences in children. A goal that states that "all children will be taught to count from one to twenty" does not take into consideration the child who is not developmentally ready to count from one to twenty. However, when the goal states that "children will be introduced to numbers from one to twenty," those who are ready are allowed to take off and those who are not ready are allowed to simply have fun with number activities.

What are the goals of your program?

Objectives offer a way to determine how and when a goal will be met. Using the goal stated above, objectives might include: "The teacher will lead the children in counting daily as they count to the day on the calendar." "At least two number activities will be played each week." "A number game will be sent home with each child at least once a month."

Through the objectives, which are, of course, objective rather than subjective, the goal will be met. When the goal is met, the purpose will be fulfilled. As goals and objectives are planned, the curriculum will unfold. Sometimes the "curriculum" is made up of ideas from the director or teacher as well as suggestions from the board of directors that allow goals to be met. Sometimes the "curriculum" is a packaged program of activities that teachers can follow and through which goals will be met.

Curriculum is more than the "quarterly guide" that is used for the weekday ministry. Planned intellectual and social stimulation is only part of the whole curriculum. Curriculum is lived out through those who relate to children. For example, a stated goal may be that "children will come to experience the love of God in their lives." The objectives for meeting this goal could be: "Teachers will greet each child by name as they arrive." "Each child will be encouraged in the activities that she or he does." "Each child will be treated by the staff as a unique and important creation of God by being spoken to and treated with respect." "Bible stories about how God has loved others will be read to the children."

The Written Curriculum

If the weekday ministry uses a written curriculum, there are a few things to keep in mind when choosing the material. Here are some key questions that need to be asked:

- Is the curriculum consistent with the values that form the purpose of the weekday ministry?
- Will the curriculum be a useful tool in meeting the goals set for the ministry?
- Is the curriculum developmentally appropriate for the variety of children the ministry will serve?
- Is the curriculum inclusive in content and language, taking into account a variety of socioeconomic levels, family styles, cultures, languages, and learning styles?
- Does the curriculum meet the needs of the children and families which the ministry serves?
- Is the curriculum easy to follow and workable in the space and time which is allotted to the weekday ministry?
- Is the curriculum compatible with the theology and Social Principles of The United Methodist Church?

Wonder-Filled Weekdays is the preschool curriculum published by the United Methodist Publishing House for Christian preschools. It contains sixty-five lessons in each of the four quarterlies. Monthly themes help to tie the activities together. Each week offers five days of activities with enough ideas to fill the day. *Wonder-Filled Weekdays* offers teachers a variety of ways to address the faith development of the children as they engage in developmentally appropriate preschool activities.

Should another "Christian" curriculum be chosen for your weekday ministry, be sure to study it carefully. The word *Christian* can easily be attached to any curriculum whether it is compatible with United Methodist theology and Social Principles or not. Use the questions above to help evaluate any curriculum being considered for the weekday ministry.

Many resource books are available with activity suggestions and ideas. Check school-supply stores and catalogs. Look in professional magazines that are published for those working in areas similar to the area for which the weekday ministry is designed. There are a number of idea magazines available that are filled with suggestions for themes and activities. For instance, *The Mailbox* magazine, published by the Education Center, offers ideas for all areas of a program as well as various age groups. This type of magazine provides ideas that can enhance almost any curriculum. Again, always measure ideas against the purposes and goals of the weekday ministry. If material is found that is not compatible, don't use it.

Curriculum Approaches

Numerous curriculum approaches exist, each highly acclaimed by those who subscribe to it. A **Theme Approach** makes use of a different topic for each month or week. All activities are designed around that theme. Popular themes for young children are families, dinosaurs, pets, community helpers, bugs, animals in winter, and space. Themes can be fun to work with, offering new ways for children to practice developmental skills.

More specific, yet less structured, than themes is the **Project Approach.** In a project approach, the children are encouraged to choose a project— a multi-stage activity exploring one particular aspect of a subject—about a topic that is of interest to them. Usually the project arises from a child's experience. For example, there may be a construction site across the street from where the weekday ministry is housed. Children are fascinated by construction sites. This may lead to a project about construction or construction machinery. Children might build a model of a construction site or create a booklet with drawings of different types of construction vehicles. The project approach is more open-ended than the theme approach. One project may last a week or six weeks, depending on the interest and involvement of the children. For more information about the project approach, check out the book *Young Investigators: The Project Approach in the Early Years,* by Judy Harris Helm and Lilian Katz (Teachers College Press, 2001).

Some people like to structure the program around a **Letter of the Week.** The letter of the week provides the theme. For example, during "A" week the children might make applesauce, hear a story about ants, paint pictures of animals, and so on. This approach is great for introducing the alphabet.

There are many more curriculum approaches. Find out what approach has worked for similar programs. You may choose to combine more than one approach or experiment until you find an approach that both fits the teaching staff and meets the purpose of the weekday ministry.

State Licensed—Church Operated

As the weekday ministry is being planned and evaluated, the board of directors will need to have a clear understanding of issues related to the separation of church and state. There will be some programs that are "open to the public" although they take place in a church building, where pictures of Jesus and quotations from the Bible are clearly part of the environment. All programs, whether specifically "Christian" in content or not, should be licensed by the state. Even if churches are exempt from licensing in your state, do all that is possible to meet and exceed licensing requirements.

The idea of the separation of church and state was instituted by the founders of this country as a safeguard for religious institutions. There is to be no national church. The church is allowed to be the church without having to follow the dictates of a national church. Likewise, the government is not accountable to any particular religious faith.

When the state issues the license for a church-operated weekday ministry, the state is providing a service to protect the church in areas of health and safety. When a church offers a weekday ministry to the general public, it is doing so as a ministry of the church. People will need to understand that, although the participants in the program may be from various faith backgrounds, the program is a ministry of a United Methodist church and they can expect the building to reflect the beliefs and traditions of United Methodism.

Licensure does not necessarily control curriculum content. Most states provide great freedom for the program to make decisions related to curriculum content. Receiving state or federal funding for a program does not necessarily restrict curriculum choices. Each funding program will have its own criteria for continued funding. Do not assume federal or state funding eliminates the possibility of Christian curriculum content.

What elements of the weekday ministry do you want the name to communicate?

A weekday program might receive funding for subsidized food, for example, that will have no impact on curriculum content provided.

Naming the Weekday Ministry

The name that is chosen for the weekday ministry will reflect a lot about the philosophy behind the program. Choose a name that reflects the purpose of the program. A name that states the location of the weekday ministry makes it clear from the title where the program takes place—for example, Forrest Avenue United Methodist Preschool or First United Methodist Daycare. These titles tell where the program is held and what kind of ministry it is. Names like these make the program easily identifiable.

There are a few things to pay attention to when choosing a name for the weekday ministry. Some names may be too cute for people to take seriously. A name like Lambs and Lollipops or Dimpled Darlings may sound sweet, but it says nothing about the purpose of the ministry. Avoid misspellings in program titles. What does a name like Kiddie Kollege Day Kare or Wee Wons Skool communicate about the academic value of the program? Pay attention to what a particular name may imply. Names can communicate a great deal about the type of curriculum or the academic quality. Notice the difference in what a name like Christian Academy for Early Learners implies in comparison to a name like God's Kid-dome.

It is also important to pay attention to anything in a name that could be misunderstood. Are there other programs using part of the same name? Could the acronym refer to something other than the weekday ministry? Keep the unchurched in mind if they are to be part of the weekday ministry. The name Matthew 19:14 Daycare has absolutely no meaning to anyone who does not already know that Matthew 19:14 says, "but Jesus said, 'Let the little children come to me, and do not stop them; for it is to such as these that the kingdom of heaven belongs.' "

WEEKDAY-MINISTRY PURPOSE WORKSHEET

Purpose Statement:
Include in the purpose who you will serve, when you will serve them, and what you will offer them.

Goals of the weekday ministry:
For each goal, write out objectives that will determine how the goal will be met.

Goal 1:

Objective:

Objective:

Objective:

Goal 2:

Objective:

Objective:

Objective:

Goal 3:

Objective:

Objective:

Objective:

Chapter Five
THE ROLE AND DUTIES
OF THE BOARD OF DIRECTORS

WEEKDAY MINISTRIES

Organizing a Board of Directors

In many situations the board of directors is the governing board of the weekday ministry. Functioning as set forth in the program bylaws, the board of directors sets policies and oversees matters of the budget, personnel, space, and program regulations.

Who Should Serve on the Board of Directors

The personalities needed on the board of directors may change as the duties move from an organizing body to a sustaining body for the weekday ministry.

An Organizing Board of Directors

An organizing body will require people who can work through the licensing process, are good at communicating, and understand how to use a purpose statement to determine goals and objectives. An organizing board may take on the responsibility of writing up the program bylaws and will need members who are experienced at this type of duty. An organizing board of directors may need to hire staff, so it will need people who are experienced in hiring and interviewing applicants. A new board will benefit from the knowledge of an accountant and an attorney. Educators can be beneficial as well.

Look at the makeup of the congregation. Churches are filled with people who, in their daily lives, practice the skills needed to establish a weekday ministry. Are there community leaders who know the needs of the surrounding area? Are there educators who are well-versed in developmentally appropriate practice in early childhood education? Are there parents who are looking for a program for their own children? Is there an accountant to help with financial information, tax issues, salaries and benefits? Is there an attorney who is knowledgeable in the area of liability? Are there others in the church who feel strongly about the need for a weekday ministry? When forming an organizing board of directors, keep in mind the necessity of the church staff, the custodian, the children's coordinator, the education ministry group, the pastor, and the director of Christian education. You may want to make some of these people ex-officio members of the board or directors—members who may be present at board meetings for input and communication but have no vote.

The makeup of an organizing board of directors might look like this:

Voting Members: Six to nine church members. One of them is a teacher, one is an attorney, one is an accountant. At least three of the members have children they are interested in enrolling in the weekday ministry.

Ex-officio members: director of weekday ministry, director of Christian education, senior pastor, church business administrator, chairperson of the church finance committee, chairperson of the board of trustees.

The Board for an Existing Weekday Ministry

The board of directors for an existing weekday ministry frequently consists of six to nine members. For example, half of them might be parents of children in the program, including some parents who are also members of the church. The remaining board members would be people from the congregation who have an energetic interest in the weekday ministry, communicate well with the surrounding community, or have demonstrated needed leadership skills.

The board of directors for an existing program will need to have a sound understanding of the purpose and history of the weekday ministry, while offering a vision of possibilities for the future. Ex-officio members may be the same as for a new board, consisting of the weekday-ministry director, the director of Christian education, the senior pastor, the chair of the education ministry group, the chair of trustees, the chair of the church finance committee, and the church business administrator. Of course all of these people are not present in every church, nor may they all need to participate in meetings of the board of directors. However, the areas of interest represented by these people will need to be continuous points for communication with the weekday ministry. The church staff should be represented through the director or other designated staff member at all board meetings.

Establishing Program Bylaws

An organizing board of directors may be the group that is responsible for establishing program bylaws, which will then be approved by the church council. The bylaws consist of articles that state the purpose and the workings of the weekday ministry.

The following is an outline for establishing bylaws. Some of the elements in the outline may or may not apply to your weekday ministry. The outline is offered as a starting place. Specifics for some of the articles contained in the bylaws are discussed in this chapter and in the rest of this manual.

SAMPLE OUTLINE FOR ESTABLISHING BYLAWS

Article I: The Name of the Organization
Article II: Purpose
Article III: The Board of Directors
      Section 1: Responsibilities
      Section 2: Number and Term of Members for the Board of Directors
      Section 3: Qualifications
      Section 4: Vacancies
      Section 5: Ex-Officio Members
      Section 6: Meetings
      Section 7: Quorum and Voting
      Section 8: Conflict of Interest
Article IV: Officers of the Board of Directors
      Section 1: Number and Term
      Section 2: Qualifications
      Section 3: Removal From Office
      Section 4: Vacancies
      Section 5: Duties of Officers
            A. Chairperson
            B. Vice-Chairperson
            C. Secretary
Article V: Director
Article VI: Committees of the Board of Directors
      Section 1: Appointment and Tenure
      Section 2: Executive Committee
            A. Appointment
            B. Responsibilities
      Section 3: Standing Committees
            A. Budget Committee
            B. Operations Committee
            C. Property and Maintenance Committee
            D. Personnel Committee
      Section 4: Quorum
Article VII: Fiscal Year
Article VIII: Budget
Article IX: Licensing
Article X: Liability Insurance
Article XI: Amendments

What qualifications should a member of the board of directors have?

Under what conditions might a member of the board of directors need to be removed from office?

How Are Board Members Elected?

Like other officers in the church, members of the board of directors are most often nominated by the church committee on lay leadership. You may want to offer some suggestions along with the director of Christian education, the pastor, or the current chairperson of the board of directors. Qualifications for board members will need to be determined and stated in the bylaws for the weekday ministry. Do members of the board of directors need to be members of the church? Can a parent whose child is in the program be a member of the board even if he or she is not a member of the church? These are questions that an establishing committee or board will need to determine.

Length of Term

It will also need to be decided how long a person can serve on the board of directors. Three classes of members who serve three-year terms would resemble other committees in the church. A board member who has served a term of three years might be eligible for an additional term or two. This would allow a person to serve up to nine consecutive years, providing consistency and a familiarity of procedure. Midterm vacancies will need to be filled. It may be decided that in the event of a midterm vacancy, you or the chairperson of the board of directors can nominate individuals for the board of directors to vote on. Conditions under which a member shall be removed from office will also need to be decided. Will attendance at meetings be mandatory? Are there any situations in which a conflict of interest might arise? How will it be determined when a board member needs to be replaced? These guidelines should be clear and easy to understand and need to be put in writing and reviewed with every new board member.

Responsibilities of the Board of Directors

The responsibilities of the board of directors may vary from church to church, depending on how the weekday ministry is structured. Generally speaking, however, most boards will share similar duties.

Setting policies is a major function of the board of directors. Policies will need to be set in relation to program operations—how enrollment is handled, guidelines for eligibility, how an enrollment waiting list is handled, and other such issues.

The board of directors is also a resource for you as program director. The board might make recommendations to you. It also acts as an element of support for you. If a family has a complaint about the weekday ministry, you can take the complaint to the board of directors and not have to deal with it alone. Conflicts are much easier to handle when they are a matter of policy rather than personality. For example, it is more effective to tell a parent that her daughter will remain on the waiting list because the policy states that enrollment is handled on a first-come, first-served basis than it is to tell her that the child will not be accepted into the program.

Besides providing support and recommendations to you and other staff, the board of directors sets policies in regard to personnel. The board must determine staff salaries and benefits. Conditions and requirements for employment will need to be made and put in writing for every staff position. Employment covenants are the responsibility of the board of directors. Policies pertaining to sick leave, personal business days, personal phone calls during weekday-ministry hours, staff dress code, vacations, and breaks will need to be established by the board. Communication between staff, church, and the community is largely the responsibility of the board. Staff need to know what is expected of them, the church needs to know how the goals of the weekday ministry are being met, and the community needs to be aware of the ministry which is being offered them.

What is expected of parents whose children participate in the weekday ministry also needs to be established by the board of directors. Will there be a late fee for families who are late paying tuition? Will there be a fee for parents who are late picking their children up? Will scholarships be available, and if so, how can parents apply for a scholarship? What forms will need to be filled out and kept on file for each participant in the weekday ministry?

Establishing goals and objectives and weighing them against the purpose of the ministry is a continual responsibility of the board of directors. Is the purpose being met? Are goals in place, and are there objectives for measuring those goals?

Weekday-ministry finances are also part of the board's responsibilities. A treasurer may be elected from the members of the board of directors to keep financial records and to write checks. Sometimes the church's financial officer or secretary takes on this responsibility, acting as an ex-officio member of the board. Financial records need to be kept for all income and expenditures. Budget preparations and an audit need to be made each year.

Issues related to property and maintenance are also a concern of the board of directors. The weekday ministry needs to be responsible for monitoring the building and the grounds which are used for the program. Fixtures and equipment need to be kept clean and in good repair. The board may decide to set up regular cleaning and repair days each quarter. On those days, board members meet on-site to deep-clean the space, equipment, and supplies that are used by the weekday ministry and to make any necessary repairs. Some repairs or cleaning needs may require recommendations to the church custodian or the church board of trustees.

Officers of the Board of Directors

Most boards of directors elect officers to care for certain tasks. The most common offices are chairperson, vice-chairperson, secretary, and treasurer.

The **chairperson** presides over the meetings of the board of directors. The chairperson is accountable to the board of directors and needs to report all pertinent information to the board. The chairperson may need to make an annual report about the weekday ministry to the church conference.

The **vice-chairperson** performs the duties of the chairperson in the chairperson's absence. A board may choose to have the vice-chairperson serve as chairperson of the budget committee or personnel committee or in another necessary capacity.

For more information on the roles and responsibilities of boards of directors, read *The Buck Stops Here: Legal and Ethical Responsibilities for United Methodist Organizations,* by Mary Logan (Discipleship Resources, 2000).

The **secretary** attends and is responsible for preparing and preserving the minutes of all board of directors meetings. The secretary may be responsible for keeping all necessary records regarding licensing and staff applications or other documents as the board determines.

The **treasurer** may be elected by the board of directors or be the church treasurer who serves as an ex-officio member of the board. This person is responsible for keeping financial records for the weekday ministry and writing checks for supplies, equipment, and other expenses. The treasurer may be given the responsibility of sending out notifications to families who are late paying tuition.

Other officers may be elected as the board of directors determines. Particular situations may require particular offices.

Incorporating

(Much of the material for this section on incorporation and tax exemption comes from a June 1, 1999, memorandum from Mary Logan and Dave Ullrich of the General Council on Finance and Administration.)

The decision to incorporate the weekday ministry as an entity separate from the rest of the church is a decision some churches choose to make. Often, the decision is made for the purpose of limitation of liability. This gives the church the ability to reduce its legal liability in matters for which the weekday ministry might be held liable—for example, an accident which injures a child or charges of unfair treatment of a member of the weekday-ministry staff. Likewise, the weekday ministry should be able to limit its own liability in the event that someone tries to hold the church liable for something.

The General Council on Finance and Administration (GCFA) does not advise every United Methodist church with a weekday ministry to either incorporate separately or not do so. Such a decision needs to reflect the church's mission in relation to the weekday ministry. There are policy and legal considerations to consider as well. In consultation with local legal counsel, the church, the weekday ministry, and the church council must consider where the church should give up control of the day-to-day operation of the weekday ministry. They might want to consider having the church act as a "parent" corporation, keeping a certain amount of control over the weekday ministry's organization as well as its assets.

Incorporation must be structured properly. If the weekday ministry does not operate as a separate organization, but instead remains in practical terms as simply a program of the church, there will be little basis for claiming limited liability in the case of a legal dispute.

The state must approve the charter of the corporation. The weekday ministry must prepare articles of incorporation and file them with the secretary of state of whichever state it will operate in.

There are a number of ways in which the church can retain control of the structure and organization of the weekday ministry. If election and removal of the ministry's board of directors remains solely the responsibility of the church, then the church will retain a basic means of control. The power to elect and remove board members can be assigned to the church in the bylaws and articles of incorporation.

Articles of Incorporation

The articles of incorporation can be prepared in a way that gives the church control over the operations of the weekday ministry. Here are some examples of provisions in the articles of incorporation that a church might want to consider (if allowed by state laws, which are not the same everywhere).

1. The church, as represented by the church council, will be the only member of the weekday-ministry corporation.
2. Only the church, being the corporation's only member, may elect and remove members of the weekday ministry's board of directors.
3. Only a member of the church may serve as director of the weekday ministry.
4. A majority of the members of the weekday ministry's board of directors must be members of the church.
5. The weekday ministry must always be in compliance with *The Book of Discipline of The United Methodist Church*.
6. The church must approve any sale or purchase of assets involving funds higher than a certain dollar amount.
7. The church must approve any change in the weekday ministry's mission or purpose.
8. The weekday ministry must obtain approval from the church to go out of business.
9. The weekday ministry must issue reports to the church on a regular basis.
10. Should the weekday ministry be dissolved, all of its assets are to become the property of the church.
11. The church must approve any changes made in the articles and bylaws of the weekday ministry.

Such provisions will give the church control of matters pertaining to the board of directors of the weekday ministry. If the weekday ministry acts in ways contrary to the church's mission and ministry, the church can dismiss any or all of the members of the board of directors. Nevertheless, the weekday ministry must remain in charge of regular proceedings, activities, and decisions. Otherwise the separate corporate status would be blurred and probably be ignored by a court.

Federal Tax-Exempt Status

A weekday ministry that is a separate corporation is not automatically tax-exempt. In general, organizations that want to claim exemption should apply for recognition of this status with the IRS during the first fifteen months of their incorporation. United Methodist local churches are tax-exempt under a group exemption with the IRS, but this ruling does not automatically include separate corporations such as weekday ministries. Weekday ministries can be included, however, if they request this status with the General Council on Finance and Administration, as long as their mission and ministry clearly support and advance the church's mission and ministry. To make such a request, the weekday ministry should write to the General Council on Finance and Administration, 1200 Davis Street, Evanston, IL 60201, Attn: Legal Department.

As an alternative to inclusion in the group ruling, a weekday ministry can file a Form 1023 application with the IRS. The IRS recognizes several primary purposes as a basis for tax exemption. The three purposes most applicable for weekday-ministry settings are (1) religious; (2) educational; and (3) charitable. To be recognized as a religious organization, the weekday ministry must have a religious focus in both its purpose and its activities and seek to instill and promote religious beliefs.

To be recognized as an educational organization, the operation of the weekday ministry should be focused on the education of the children in the program. Teachers will need to be highly trained in education. Organizations that provide childcare so that parents may maintain employment also qualify as educational organizations when they are open to the general public.

To be recognized as a charitable organization, the weekday ministry must focus on caring for children whose needs would otherwise go unmet, as by offering childcare to low-income families at reduced or no fees or by providing special care for children in disadvantaged families.

In many states, once the weekday ministry receives exemption from federal income taxation, it is automatically exempt from state income tax. If not, the weekday ministry will need to file for state income tax exemption with the proper state agency.

Other Steps Related to Incorporation

There are other steps that will need to be taken, including the following.

1. The weekday ministry must obtain an employer identification number. This requires completing and filing Form SS-4 from the Internal Revenue Service.
2. Weekday-ministry bylaws must be drafted.
3. Church bylaws must be changed to explain the relationship between the church and the weekday ministry.
4. Church assets that will be used to operate the weekday ministry may be transferred to the weekday-ministry corporation. This might include such things as bank accounts that the weekday ministry will draw from. The GCFA advises churches to create a lease and charge rent for buildings or land that the separately incorporated weekday ministry will use. The church should have an attorney prepare the lease, which should clearly state what the financial arrangements will be, what the weekday ministry's hours of operation will be, and what the rights and limitations of access to the property are.
5. The weekday ministry must acquire liability and property insurance separate from the church's.
6. The weekday ministry may need to arrange for worker's compensation insurance for its employees. Worker's compensation depends on state law, so regulations may vary by state.
7. There must be a separate board of directors for the weekday ministry. This board must elect officers and be ready to hold meetings and keep records current.
8. The weekday ministry, in most states, must file an annual report (separate from the church's) with the secretary of state of the state where the weekday ministry operates.

9. The weekday ministry must keep its own books and records, separate from the church's.
10. The weekday ministry needs to learn about and comply with state laws regarding federal unemployment tax.
11. The weekday ministry must establish an employee payroll separate from the church's. All federal and state employment tax returns and other tax information must also be filed separately by the weekday ministry.
12. If a weekday ministry has applied to the IRS for tax-exempt status instead of receiving coverage under the group ruling for the denomination, federal tax Form 990 may be required if the weekday ministry's annual receipts total more than $25,000. The IRS may require this return even if the organization does not have to pay any tax.
13. Weekday ministries must have clearly stated, written personnel policies. There should be policies on hiring practices, wages and benefits, vacation time, sick leave, hours of work, religious requirements, performance reviews, discipline, termination and resignation, sexual harassment, racism, and child safety.
14. A weekday ministry must also obey federal, state, and local regulations on numerous other issues. These may include zoning laws and building codes for schools and childcare; laws concerning upkeep of the weekday ministry's property; standards for providing reasonable access into and within buildings to people who are disabled; guidelines for proper screening of employees; and laws concerning child abuse, including what steps must be taken to prevent it and what must be done to report it if it occurs. Many of these topics are covered in the licensing process.

As the governing body of the weekday ministry, the board of directors will operate at a different level if a program is a separate incorporation. Always keep in mind the purpose of the ministry and your role of servant leadership.

Chapter Six
FAITHFUL FINANCING

WEEKDAY MINISTRIES

The Monetary Cost of a Weekday Ministry

Quality weekday ministries cost money. They cost money to set up and they cost money to sustain. Weekday ministries are never a fundraising opportunity to provide easy funds for the local church.

Setting Up a Start-Up Budget

Setting up a start-up budget is one of the first tasks of a board of directors or weekday-ministry committee. The start-up budget should include line items for every expense and need imaginable for the weekday ministry. It should also include sources of income.

An Operating Budget

An operating budget is similar to a start-up budget but has more particulars in place. The first year or two are the most difficult to determine expenses and income for, but a start-up budget is necessary for program approval by a church administrative body such as the church council. The church needs to know what expenses are involved and what income is available. Also, if the weekday ministry applies for nonprofit status as a separate organization, a start-up budget will be requested as part of the application.

Once the weekday ministry is in place, registration fees and tuition usually become the main source of income. Sometimes, in order to get the ministry off to a good start, funds are needed from other sources.

Non-Tuition Funding

Non-tuition funding can come from many sources. Donations, fundraising, and interest on investments and accounts are all non-tuition funding

List sources of income currently available to your program.

sources. Foundations and grants are another form of non-tuition funding. Begin by seeking grants from local organizations and foundations. Ask around. There are many grants available that most people know nothing about. Check with your annual conference office and with your local resource and referral agency. Every state has an association for nonprofits that can be an excellent aid in seeking funding sources. The Foundation Center of New York publishes *The Foundation Directory*, which most libraries have on hand. They also have a website at www.fdncenter.org.

Every funder has a different form of grant proposal. When writing a grant proposal, keep the goal of the grant maker in mind. If you are seeking a grant from a health foundation, emphasize how your weekday ministry will improve the health and development of children and their families. If the funder is an educational foundation, focus on the educational purpose of the weekday ministry. Design a proposal that is a good fit between the grant maker and your weekday ministry. Writing grant proposals can be a tedious job, but if your proposal is accepted, it will enrich your weekday ministry and open up new possibilities.

Responsible Fundraising

Fundraising events are another source for income. Fundraising can be an enjoyable way for everyone to contribute to the weekday ministry. Listed below are some fundraising events. Be creative as you and the board of directors explore other possible fundraising activities.

Bake Sale: Everyone likes to eat.

Fun Night at Church: Have a carnival at church involving every class and organization. Each group can be in charge of a booth. Booth suggestions might include: cake walk, face painting, fish pond, dunking booth, hat-making contest, petting zoo, pocket clown with surprises for children in big pockets. The possibilities are endless.

Dinners: Again, everyone likes to eat. Soup suppers, spaghetti dinners, and pancake feeds are common. Other possibilities exist as you explore community festivals or ethnic celebrations. An Irish potato bar around St. Patrick's day or a bierocks supper as part of a community Oktoberfest would not only serve as a fundraiser for the weekday ministry but also add to the festive mood of the community.

Penny Drive: Set up a container in each Sunday school class to collect pennies for the weekday ministry.

A-Thons: Bike-a-thon, hop-a-thon, rock-a-thon. This type of fundraiser promotes physical activity as well as community involvement.

Children's Clothing Exchange: Have a place for parents to bring the clothes their children have outgrown. Put a small price on each item, and other parents can find some nice, inexpensive clothes and contribute to the weekday ministry as well.

Play-Dough Sale: Make homemade play-dough. Have parents help make and package the play-dough. Sell it to families, other classes, perhaps even other schools.

Recipe Book Variation: Have each child bring a recipe or two from home. Print the recipe on one page and then the child's directions for making the dish on the other page.

Recipes For Kids: Put together a book with recipes for play dough, gooey mixture, soap-flake molding compound, and fun foods kids like to eat. Be sure to make it plain which things can be eaten and which cannot!

Breakfast With Santa: Sponsor a Breakfast With Santa and have families buy tickets to come for a nice breakfast and to meet Santa.

The ideas are endless, from the old reliable rummage sales to something no one has ever thought about before. Be sure that fundraising events uphold the beliefs and practices of The United Methodist Church. For example, the Social Principles, which are found in *The Book of Discipline*, state: "The Church should promote standards and personal lifestyles that would make unnecessary and undesirable the resort to commercial gambling—including public lotteries—as a recreation, as an escape, or as a means of producing public revenue or funds for support of charities or government" (From *The Book of Discipline of The United Methodist Church—2000.* Copyright © 2000 by The United Methodist Publishing House; ¶ 163, page 115. Used by permission.). Therefore, to hold a lottery or a raffle as a fundraising event would be inappropriate, as they set up "chance" giving. Ticket sales, however, offer an event where everyone receives the same benefits with no chance to win or lose.

So-called "Slave Auctions" have been used as fundraisers by some organizations. More appropriate would be a "Give-and-Take" event where one person might say, "I will provide three nights of babysitting for you if you donate the amount you would pay me to the weekday-ministry program."

Money Management Options

When it comes to managing the finances of a weekday ministry, it is best to keep it simple and build in checks and balances. A program that is built within the existing structure of the church may have a budget incorporated in the larger church budget. More typically, the weekday ministry will be self-supporting in that it will have its own board of directors and officers and its own budget and financial records. This is similar to groups in the church like United Methodist Women or United Methodist Men. These groups exist within the church but frequently have a structure of their own that includes a budget and financial bookkeeping.

Money handling needs to be addressed. Who handles the money that is received and spent for the weekday ministry? If yours is a small program that employs one or two people, the process will be fairly simple. As enrollment and tuition fees are received, the program director will record them, make out carbon or computer receipts, and deposit them into the bank account. As money is used for the program, records and canceled checks are filed. The account is balanced at least monthly, a report is made to the board of directors at a regularly scheduled time, and an annual audit of the weekday-ministry books is completed.

Some boards of directors elect a treasurer to keep track of the financial records. All checks are handed over to the treasurer, who records and deposits them. Receipts of expenditures are turned in to the treasurer for approval by the board and reimbursement from the program funds. It is strongly recommended that the check-signing procedures require two signatures.

Outline your program's procedures for receiving and disbursing funds. What checks and balances are in place?

Larger programs may be more complicated. Yet no matter how large the program is, the fewer hands through which money passes, the better.

Tuition and Fees

Determining tuition and fees for the weekday ministry will depend on the type of program being offered. You will need to decide whether to charge hourly, weekly, or monthly rates. Find out what similar programs in your area are charging and start from there. Consider the services being offered. Is a meal being served? Is the program providing most or all of the supplies? Is transportation to and from school provided by the weekday ministry? All of these things will be part of the necessary fees.

It will also need to be determined what is equitable for those being served by the weekday ministry. If the ministry is primarily to lower-income families, then the fees need to reflect what people are able to pay. Some churches provide a sliding scale, depending on income level. In other places, children from lower-income families qualify for a Head Start program, so the ministry serves families who would not qualify for such programs.

Scholarships

Offering scholarships to children whose families would have difficulty paying full tuition is another option. Sometimes scholarship money will be donated by community service organizations. Scholarship money can also be the goal for a fundraiser. What percentage of the full tuition cost the scholarship will cover may depend on the available funds.

Determining who qualifies for a scholarship can sometimes be a tricky matter. One church may determine scholarship need by obtaining a copy of the state income levels that allow children to receive a free school lunch. This method requires that the director have access to family income-tax-return forms. Another church may have a worksheet for families to provide household income levels. Others may simply ask families for an amount they feel they could comfortably pay and go with it, provided the scholarship money is available to cover the remainder. You will need to decide what is fair in your situation. Consider equitable treatment of the children you serve as well as the staff providing the service. Most churches do not want children to miss out on quality childcare or an early childhood educational opportunity simply because a family cannot afford it.

Staff Salaries

Childcare providers are traditionally underpaid. This is partly because of the need to keep tuition and fees at a rate that families can afford. At the same time, it is important as the church to affirm the value of the staff, their God-given gifts, and their education and training. Compare what other programs in your area are paying their staffs. You may have full-time staff and part-time staff. You may need the assistance of volunteers as you begin your ministry. Even volunteers need to be compensated in some way, be it formal recognition, appreciation events, or frequent notes of thanks.

As you determine your staff salaries, you will need to decide what benefits will be offered. For a full-time staff person, heath insurance should be an option. Check with your annual conference to see if you can add weekday-ministry staff to the health insurance plan offered to the clergy and other church staff. As an alternative, some insurance companies have reasonable rates for small businesses.

Other Benefits

Other benefits may include pension, paid vacation time, sick leave, and social security. You may need to start with sick leave and paid vacation time. As the weekday ministry grows, your staff benefits can grow with it. Even at the early stages of developing the weekday ministry, check into all of these benefits so that the church can offer the most equitable package possible to the staff of the weekday ministry.

As the director of the weekday-ministry program, you may find yourself in a position to raise the issue of salary or benefits for your staff or yourself. This issue is seldom easy to address. However, if the quality of the program is jeopardized by the salary of staff members, it's time to speak up. There may be a constant struggle with trying to offer a salary that is equal to the educational level and time commitment you need for the quality program you would like to provide. When you find that the salary is not attracting the educated or experienced people needed for the staff, something will need to be done to increase the salary. Likewise, if staff salaries are below those of similar programs in your area, a change will need to be made.

Asking for a Raise

When the time comes to ask for a staff raise, there are three things to keep in mind. (1) Gather information, comparing salaries of similar positions in your area. Compile the information in a form that is easy to interpret at a glance. (2) Find support among members of the board of directors. Speak with individuals who are familiar with your qualifications and time commitment. Speak with individuals who may not be aware of your qualifications or the comparative salaries of your peers. (3) Make your presentation to the board of directors with confidence. Have your facts straight and in a prepared form to hand out to the board. Keep a focus on the mission of the weekday ministry rather than on how deserving you are of a raise. You want the weekday ministry to be as strong as possible, and in order for this to happen, the staff must be affirmed and supported.

What benefits do you currently offer staff?

How do your staff's wages compare with those paid by other programs in the area?

Are staff who work full-time in your program making a wage that allows them to live above the poverty line?

SAMPLE START-UP BUDGET

Mission Valley United Methodist Church
Mission Valley Preschool

(This budget is based on a particular number of participants as indicated by interest
inventories and registration.)

	Amount
Employee Expenses	
Teacher Continuing Education Fees	_____
Salaries	_____
Social Security/Worker's Compensation	_____
Staff Training	
Membership in NAEYC	_____
(Other Employee Expenses and Benefits)	_____
Operating Expenses	
Licensing Fees	_____
Supplies/Equipment/Furniture	_____
Food	_____
Transportation	_____
Copy Machine Expenses	_____
Postage and Delivery	_____
End of Year Celebration Supper	_____
Audit	_____
Liability Insurance	_____
Telephone Directory Ad	_____
(Other Operating Expenses)	_____
Property Expenses	
Utilities	_____
Fire Alarm Installation (for the trustees)	_____
Janitorial Supplies and Labor	_____
Telephone	_____
(Other Property Expenses)	_____
Income	
Start-up Grant	_____
Tuition	_____
Registration Fees	_____
Church Special Offering	_____
Fundraiser Event	_____

Chapter Seven
STAFF DEVELOPMENT

WEEKDAY MINISTRIES

Hiring Staff

Hiring and supervising staff is one of the most important responsibilities of the weekday-ministry director. The quality of the program is dependent upon having excellent staff who care deeply about children and who are continuously learning from their experiences and increasing their skills and knowledge.

No matter who the applicant is, the same process should be followed for hiring staff. Whether the individual is a long-time member of the church, clergy, or a total stranger, the process should unfold with the submission of an application, a complete interview, a child-abuse and criminal-background check, a completed health form, and the signing of an employee covenant.

Hiring the Director

Often, the director of the weekday ministry is hired by the staff-parish relations committee, since this person is considered to be part of the church staff. Like others on the church staff, the director is accountable to the staff-parish relations committee for annual evaluations and concerns related to the job description. In other churches, the director is hired by the weekday-ministry board of directors. In this situation, the director would be accountable to the board of directors. The filling of other staff positions is usually the job of the weekday-ministry director and the board of directors.

When a new program begins, the director of the weekday ministry is usually the first person to be hired. This can come about in a number of ways. Sometimes the director is the person who presented the idea of the weekday ministry to the church. This is usually someone who has had experience in childcare or Christian education and shares a vision of such ministry with the church. Other times, the director's position is assumed by an existing member of the church staff, often the director of Christian education or the children's minister. In other situations, the church hires someone to fill the position. This entails setting up a job description, taking applications, and interviewing candidates. Interviews take place with the staff-parish relations committee and/or the weekday-ministry board of directors.

Fairness in Hiring

Fairness should be practiced throughout the hiring process.

Federal laws prohibit employment discrimination based on race, color, religion, gender, national origin, age, or disabilities. You, along with the board of directors, will need to decide what qualifications are needed for staff positions and state them as clearly as possible in the job description. There may be certain physical disabilities that would make it difficult for someone to work with young children. Therefore, it should be stated that one of the qualifications for the position is that the person must be physically able to speak to children at a child's eye level and have the ability to assist children with toileting and other health and safety needs. Any religious requirements need to be made clear as well. As a ministry of the church, you may decide that every staff member should hold basic Christian beliefs or be a member of a United Methodist church.

Job Descriptions

A job description needs to be provided for each position. Usually the responsibility of developing the job description for the director lies with the board of directors or governing body of the weekday ministry. Job descriptions for teachers and other staff of the weekday ministry are often developed by the director with consultation and approval from the board of directors. Job descriptions should be clear and concise, stating the qualifications needed, the responsibilities that go with the position, and to whom the person is accountable.

The Job Application

Application forms need to be brief and informative enough to determine which applicants warrant an interview. Basic personal information, a brief educational and employment history, and a list of references will usually suffice.

Along with the application form, an application packet should include a health form (usually provided by the licensing agency) and the job description.

The Interview

The interview should be handled with as much fairness as possible. A standard set of interview questions and the same interview committee for each applicant will make the interview process more fair.

Before any applicants are interviewed, the director and the board of directors should determine what information is desired by the end of the interview. Use the goals of the ministry and the job description as a guide.

Using that information, draw up a set of standard questions to be used with each applicant during the interview process. An interview checklist should also be written.

Along with the checklist and the standard interview questions, all the necessary information ought to be at hand so that you can conduct an efficient interview. You will need the following forms:

- Interview Checklist
- Interview Questions
- Application
- List of References
- Job Description
- Salary Information

Background Checks

No one should ever be hired without a criminal-background check and a child-abuse-history check. The child-abuse check is often done by the state licensing agency, and a form will be provided in the licensing packet. A criminal check can be done with the assistance of the state police department or by a reputable agency. Follow your state guidelines.

The Health Form

A health form is also usually provided by the state licensing agency. Everyone who works with children in the weekday ministry will need to have a physical examination by a physician or the county health nurse. The physical examination will need to include a current tuberculin test.

Employment Covenant

An "employment covenant" describes that which the church offers an employee. The employment covenant states the privileges and the responsibilities of the parties involved. For example, a privilege of the employee is to have two weeks paid vacation each year. A responsibility is to arrive at work fifteen minutes before the children arrive. A privilege of the church is to be able to offer a ministry for children during the weekday. A responsibility is to ensure upkeep and repair of the space provided for the weekday ministry.

The employee covenant is a useful tool. It can serve as a reference when job expectations are not met. It can be used as a negotiation tool at the annual staff assessment. Regular review of the covenant can reveal issues that need to be discussed by the board of directors and the staff of the weekday ministry.

Continued Supervision

Staff Training

Staff training is an essential part of building an effective staff for ministry. It can serve not only to provide education and the required continuing education experiences but also to build rapport among the staff members. Training events help staff to develop a common understanding of the purpose and philosophy of the weekday ministry and can serve to open lines of communication.

Staff training can take many forms, from orientations at the beginning of the year for a new staff to planning and evaluation sessions. A training event could take place in an evening meeting, on a weekend, or in a retreat setting. Sometimes staff training will focus on a single topic that is applicable to the weekday ministry.

Some Possible Staff Training Event Topics
- First Aid and CPR
- Recognizing and Reporting Child Abuse
- Exploring Math and Science With Preschoolers
- Puppetry
- Helping Children Deal With Grief
- Positive Discipline
- Spanish Classes
- Children With Special Needs
- Exploring Creative Arts
- Brain Development in Infants and Toddlers
- Faith Development With Young Children
- Using Prayer in the Classroom

Tap the expertise of people in your community or in the annual conference to provide inspiration and information about a particular topic. Attendance at some of these training events can be extended to the rest of the congregation. For example, first-aid or Spanish classes can serve to educate not only the weekday-ministry staff but other interested church members as well.

Educating the Larger Staff

Those hired by the director or the board of directors may be considered the weekday-ministry staff, but in reality a larger staff exists among the congregation and the families that make the program work. The church staff needs to have a firm understanding of the ministry that takes place during the week and how Jesus Christ lives through it. When people call the church office to inquire, whoever answers the telephone needs to have the information readily available and to be able to articulate it with ease.

Informal and formal reports to the church staff, newsletters, bulletin and pulpit announcements, newspaper articles, and project displays are all ways of educating others about the weekday ministry.

Through your participation in church staff meetings and in other interaction with staff members, you have the opportunity to educate the entire church staff about the needs of the children and families you serve. There are many ways to educate the larger staff about the weekday ministry and how Christ's love is working through it. That is part of your servant leadership role.

Staff Reviews

A supervisor's responsibility is to enable staff members to do their jobs in the most effective way possible. Staff supervision includes both continuing interaction with staff, in which you provide ongoing information and feedback, and regularly scheduled opportunities for evaluation and goal-setting.

Formal reviews should be done at least annually. For new staff members there should be a review after an initial probationary period. Staff reviews provide an opportunity to recognize goals that have been met, to hear staff hopes and concerns regarding their positions, and to develop new goals. An evaluation form summarizing goals agreed upon and items discussed should be signed by both the staff member and the supervisor and be retained in the staff member's personnel file.

When Staff Leave

Exit Interview

When staff resign it is advisable to have an exit interview. This provides an opportunity to affirm the contributions the staff member has made and to discuss suggestions that they have for improving the program. Sometimes during an exit interview staff will reveal very important information that they might not have felt comfortable discussing before.

The exit interview also provides a time to make sure all paperwork is in order and that any keys, staff identification cards, and so forth are returned.

Firing a Staff Member

When a staff member is not carrying out the responsibilities as stated in the employee covenant or the job descriptions, something needs to be done. A process should be in place so that when the situation arises, those involved will have a procedure to follow.

When a staff member is not fulfilling job requirements, the director needs to approach that person with the concern. In consultation with the board of directors, the staff person may be given a period of time in which improvement will need to take place. If improvement is made, then the situation has been remedied. If no improvement is apparent, then the covenant has been broken and that person will be removed.

It is important to document conversations you have with the staff member. It is advisable for both yourself and the staff member to sign and date the documentation.

Keep the chairperson of the board of directors or governing body informed at each step of the process of terminating a staff member.

SAMPLE JOB DESCRIPTION
Preschool Director

Qualifications

1. Meet the state-required qualifications for preschool director.

2. Have a friendly, open personality.

3. Enjoy working with children ages three to five.

4. Hold membership in a United Methodist church.

5. Be physically and emotionally equipped to work with young children.

6. Hold current CPR and first-aid certification.

7. Be a member of the National Association for the Education of Young Children.

Responsibilities

1. Plan and implement a preschool program for children ages three to five that is developmentally appropriate and helps children develop physically, cognitively, emotionally, socially, and spiritually.

2. Receive and review applications for other staff positions, interview candidates, and make hiring recommendations to the board of directors.

3. Train other staff in accordance with the goals of the preschool.

4. Receive and record tuition payments before turning them over to the treasurer of the board of directors.

5. Evaluate staff annually.

6. Communicate with the congregation about events and activities that are taking place in preschool.

7. Receive enrollment packets and make sure that each child has all the necessary enrollment forms completed.

8. Communicate with parents about any concerns the staff may have about their child.

9. Receive at least ten contact hours of continuing education annually as approved by the state licensing agency.

Accountabilities

1. Meet with the board of directors every other month.

2. Attend weekly church staff meetings.

3. Make a report to the church conference annually.

4. Meet with staff-parish relations committee annually or as requested.

SAMPLE JOB APPLICATION
Preschool Teacher

First Name _____ MI _____ Last Name _____

Date of Birth _____

Street Address _____

City _____ State _____ Zip Code _____

Daytime Phone _____ Evening Phone _____

E-mail address _____

Social Security # _____

Education (Start with the most recent):

School	Major	Dates Attended	Degree

Employment History (Start with the most recent):

Name of Employer	Duties	Dates

References: (Include your previous employer and two people who have known you for at least three years.)

Name (Relationship)	Address	Telephone

SAMPLE INTERVIEW QUESTIONS AND CHECKLIST
Preschool Teacher

Questions

1. What experience have you had teaching children ages three to five?

2. What strengths do you bring to this job?

3. In what areas could we help you grow?

4. What is your understanding of developmentally appropriate practice?

5. Tell us about your philosophy of early childhood education.

6. What would you do if one child bit another child?

7. How would you approach parents with a concern about their child?

8. What experience do you have with The United Methodist Church?

9. What kind of training do you have in early childhood education?

10. What experience have you had with faith formation and preschool children?

11. What questions or concerns do you have about the church or the preschool as a ministry of the church?

Checklist

Key:

1–Exceeds Expectations	2–Meets Expectations
3–Some Improvement Needed	4–Much Improvement Needed

Appears well-groomed	1	2	3	4
Pleasant personality	1	2	3	4
Appeared at ease during interview	1	2	3	4
Communication skills	1	2	3	4
Self-confidence	1	2	3	4
Knowledgeable about				
The United Methodist Church	1	2	3	4
Preschool education	1	2	3	4
Faith formation in children	1	2	3	4
Other job-related issues	1	2	3	4
Motivation	1	2	3	4
Job experience	1	2	3	4
Education and training	1	2	3	4
Openness to questions and suggestions	1	2	3	4

Qualifications

1. Possess a friendly personality.

2. Enjoy working with children ages three to five.

3. Be physically and emotionally equipped to work with young children.

4. Meet the state licensing educational requirements.

5. Hold a current first-aid certificate and a certificate from a training seminar on reporting child abuse.

Responsibilities

1. Demonstrate Christian love to children, families, and other staff members.

2. Supervise the day-to-day activities of the preschool class by:
   a. planning developmentally appropriate activities that meet the program goals and objectives.
   b. setting up learning centers each week in the areas of math or reading readiness, art, the physical senses, discovery (science or social studies), dramatic play, and gross motor development.
   c. remaining with the children at all times.

3. Enforce health and safety practices by:
   a. intervening when a child's activity may result in injury.
   b. following licensing procedures to safeguard the health and safety of children—hand-washing, sanitation of toys and equipment, playground safety rules, and rules regarding the use of supplies and equipment.
   c. being knowledgeable about emergency procedures and presenting to the preschool director a completed accident or illness report for each incident.
   d. carrying out and recording monthly fire and tornado drills.
   e. reporting any suspicions of child abuse to the preschool director.

4. Assist the preschool director in preparing program materials.

5. Discuss any difficult child behavior with the preschool director.

6. Assist children with self-help skills.

7. Arrive at least 15 minutes before class begins and stay until the last child has been picked up.

8. Receive 6 hours of continuing education each year as approved by the director.

9. Attend staff training events as required by the director.

10. Abide by policies and procedures as outlined in the employee handbook.

Accountabilities

1. Be accountable to the preschool director.

2. Fill out a progress report three times a year for each child.

3. Conduct parent-teacher conferences each October and April.

SAMPLE JOB COVENANT

Responsibilities of the Preschool Director

1. The preschool director will carry out responsibilities as listed on the job description.
2. If the preschool director has concerns regarding his or her stated responsibilities, the preschool director will discuss them with the board of directors.
3. The preschool director will serve in this position from August 1 until May 15, at which time the covenant will be reviewed for renewal.
4. Should a situation arise which would make it impossible or undesirable to serve until the stated date, the preschool director should give a three-week notice in writing to the chairperson of the board of directors.
5. The preschool director will respect the sanctity of the church space, time, and furnishings.

Privileges of the Preschool Director

1. The preschool director will receive a total salary of _____ for the preschool year.
2. The preschool director will be paid a portion of that salary every two weeks, with appropriate IRS and social security withholding.
3. Vacations of the preschool director will coincide with preschool vacations as indicated on the calendar in the employee handbook.
4. A total of five sick days/personal-business days are allowed to the preschool director during the preschool year. Additional days will be deducted from the salary.

Responsibilities of the Local Church

1. The local church will provide a budget from which the preschool director may purchase necessary equipment and supplies.
2. The local church will provide janitorial and maintenance upkeep for the preschool rooms and outdoor play area.
3. The local church will promote awareness of the preschool through the church newsletter, bulletins, and local newspaper.
4. The local church will pay an annual salary of _____, which will be given in two-week increments throughout the preschool year.
5. The local church will listen to concerns of the preschool director through the board of directors.
6. In the event that the preschool director is not upholding his or her responsibilities as stated in this covenant, the board of directors will inform the preschool director of necessary changes. If improvement has not been noted within two weeks of written notification, the preschool director will be placed on a two-week probation period. If after this time changes still have not been made to the satisfaction of the board of directors, the covenant will be considered broken and the preschool director will be dismissed from this position.

Privileges of the Local Church

1. The local church will have the ability to offer this ministry to young children.
2. The local church will celebrate activities and milestones of the preschool in worship and in publications.
3. The local church will reach out to families in the community.

I, _____, on this date _____, do enter this covenant with the Mission Valley United Methodist Church, having read and understood the privileges and responsibilities of myself as preschool director, and of the church as the organization through which the ministry entitled Mission Valley Preschool is offered.

I, _____, as chairperson of the board of directors of the Mission Valley United Methodist Church Preschool, on this date _____, do enter this covenant with _____, having read and understood the privileges and responsibilities of the Mission Valley United Methodist Church and of _____ as the preschool director.

Chapter Eight
HANDBOOKS

Handbooks can be a crucial tool for the weekday ministry. They provide a place to print policies and procedures. Handbooks answer many questions that would otherwise require a verbal response to every person involved in the program. Handbooks are also useful as a way to introduce the weekday ministry to people beyond the local church. When someone outside of the congregation asks about the weekday ministry, a parent's handbook may be the most complete way to share information.

Types of Handbooks

Three types of handbooks are useful for a weekday ministry. The *parent's handbook* is written to share information that parents of children in the program need to know. It serves as a reference for parents throughout the year. A parent's handbook is a document of printed policies for parents.

An *employee handbook* covers information that employees of the weekday ministry need to know. Policies and procedures related to staff and expectations of staff are documented in the employee handbook.

An *operations manual* for the board of directors serves as a printed policy document for people serving on the board of directors of the weekday ministry. It can be an educational tool for new board members, a duty list for officers, and an outline of the responsibilities of the board and the policies which the board is called to evaluate and uphold.

What to Include in a Parent Handbook

A parent handbook is a tool for informing parents about the weekday ministry. A mission statement or statement of purpose should always be included and printed in a way that will catch the reader's attention. The mission statement could be printed on the front cover of the handbook or just inside the front cover, where it is set apart from the rest of the text. A mission statement or purpose statement is the "why" of the program. It communicates in a clear, concise way what the weekday ministry is all about.

> The purpose of the Mission Valley Preschool is to provide an informal learning atmosphere in which children will grow physically, mentally, socially, emotionally, and spiritually through developmentally appropriate activities in order to develop a positive self-image and prepare them for the transition into kindergarten.

Also in the handbook will be a statement that describes what the program does. The "what" of the program consists of services that are provided through the weekday ministry. Services include that which is the focus of the program and who the program is designed to serve.

> Mission Valley Preschool is a ministry of the Mission Valley United Methodist Church and serves children from age three to the age of kindergarten eligibility. It is a half-day program and is licensed by the state. Children must be three years old by September 1st and must be toilet trained. It is strongly encouraged that all children be screened through the special-education department at Belmont Elementary School before enrolling in preschool.

The parent handbook is a place to list the goals and objectives of the weekday ministry. Include that which the program hopes to accomplish and how these goals will be met.

> Children will grow socially and emotionally by learning to . . .
> - listen
> - follow simple directions
> - think for themselves
> - live within limits they can understand
> - make choices
> - express feelings in socially acceptable ways
> - identify with an adult other than a parent
> - feel secure away from home
> - make new friends
> - work both individually and in a group
> - take turns
> - share
>
> Children will grow physically and mentally by . . .
> - developing large and small muscle coordination
> - developing visual and auditory discrimination
> - developing language skills
> - recognizing colors and shapes
> - recognizing uppercase and some lowercase letters
> - recognizing and writing numbers 1 to 10
> - working creatively with the hands
> - learning to cut with scissors
>
> Children will grow spiritually by . . .
> - practicing prayer at meals and snacks
> - hearing age-appropriate Bible stories

- exploring God's wonderful creation
- celebrating major Christian holidays
- hearing faith language such as *God, prayer, Jesus, love,* and *worship* used in the classroom

These goals are built into the preschool curriculum. The curriculum is a mixture of play, stories, songs, movement, activities, art, and learning projects.

Specifics of the weekday ministry should be spelled out in the parent handbook. This is the place to address the questions parents might have about the program. Information should be organized in a way that makes it easy for parents to look up information when they have a question. Topic headings are useful.

Tuition and Fees

1. A $50.00 enrollment fee is paid at the time of enrollment and goes toward accident insurance and supplies.
2. Tuition rates for August to May average out to $8.00 per day. Monthly tuition for the three-day-a-week program is $96.00. Monthly tuition for the five-day-a-week program is $160.00.
3. Tuition can be paid semiannually in August and in January or each month. Tuition is due the first preschool day of each month.
4. A $5.00 late fee will be added for tuition that is not paid by the tenth day of the month. The child of anyone failing to pay tuition by the twentieth day of the month will have to be dismissed.
5. No refunds of tuition can be made for a child who is withdrawn during the month.
6. No refunds can be made in the case of vacations or absenteeism, except in emergency cases where a doctor recommends a long convalescence. Plans are made for your child whether he or she is here or not.
7. Should inclement weather force a closing of the city's public schools, Mission Valley Preschool will be closed as well. Five extra snow days have been built into the preschool calendar.

Enrollment

Mission Valley Preschool does not discriminate on the basis of national origin, ancestry, or gender, in accordance with state law. Christian values and attitudes will be practiced, although specific religious doctrine is not a major emphasis of the curriculum.

The state requires the following forms to be completed before a child can enter Mission Valley Preschool: (1) A medical record for each child to be filled out by parents and either the child's doctor or the public health nurse. This form includes a medical history, record of immunizations, and a physical examination and screening tests. (2) A permission slip that is to be signed by parents for field trips, for pictures taken for publicity purposes, and for transfer of records. (3) An emergency release for medical treatment, which is to be signed by parents in case the parent cannot be reached during a medical emergency requiring the care of a doctor or hospital. Forms can be obtained from the preschool director or picked up at the church office. An Enrollment Open House will take place on August 16th from 8:30 A.M. to 11:30 A.M. and from 5:30 P.M. to 7:30 P.M. Parents are encouraged to bring their child to the preschool rooms sometime during these hours to meet the teachers, see the preschool rooms, and turn in enrollment papers.

List the goals and objectives for your weekday ministry.

What questions do parents frequently ask?

Preschool Hours and Attendance

1. Sessions are held Monday through Friday from 9:00 A.M. to 11:30 A.M.
2. Preschool starts at 9:00 A.M. Please try to get your child to preschool as close to the starting time as possible. Children may arrive 5 minutes before class begins, but 10 minutes is too early. Early arrival makes the first activity too long for a young child and interrupts teacher preparation time.
3. Pick up your child promptly at dismissal time. It is upsetting to a child to be left after other children have gone.
4. When bringing your children to preschool and picking them up afterward, please enter through the east door of the church and walk with your child to and from the preschool room door.
5. If someone other than a designated person is to call for your child, the parent should notify the preschool director in advance. Children will only be released to people who have been designated to pick them up.
6. Please call if your child will be missing school.
7. Please keep your child home if any of the following symptoms are present: stomach upset due to nausea, vomiting, rash, fever, frequent stools, bad cough, sore throat, or eyes that show infection.
8. If your child is on medication, please notify the preschool director.

Discipline Policy

Mission Valley Preschool seeks to demonstrate positive guidance for children. There are a few simple rules and a consistent reminder to children who "forget" the rules. Often, a reminder is all it takes to change a child's behavior. Staff will speak calmly to the child about how the behavior was inappropriate. If a child becomes uncontrollably distractive to the other children, a parent will be contacted to come and take the child home for the remainder of the session. In consultation with the parent, the director may work out a behavior modification plan for a child.

Emergency Procedures

In case of fire, children will be ushered out the east door of the church and meet at the far end of the parking lot. Fire drills will be held once a month.

In the event of a tornado, children will be ushered to the hallway in the education wing of the church. Tornado drills will be held in the months of August, September, April, and May.

In the event of a serious injury or illness, parents will be contacted. If a trip to the emergency room is necessary, the director will accompany the child to the hospital while the teaching assistant stays with the rest of the children at the church. An accident or illness report will be filled out and kept on file.

Snacks

Snacks will be served mid-morning. Snacks will consist of at least two food groups. Children will be introduced to a variety of foods during snack time. Often, they will participate in the preparation of the snacks. Handwashing will always be practiced before preparing or eating snacks.

Security Measures

In order to keep children safe, security measures will be practiced. Mission Valley Preschool staff and volunteers will wear identifying nametags. Children will be signed in upon their arrival on the sign-in board just outside the preschool room. Children will be signed out as they leave each day. Although there is an open-door policy to allow parents to drop by and visit preschool anytime, only authorized parents or family will be allowed to come to preschool. Unauthorized people will not be allowed inside the preschool room. Video cameras are in place at all entrances of the church so church staff can monitor those who come and go during preschool hours.

Weather Policy

Please dress children in casual, comfortable, and washable clothes that are appropriate for the weather. Old clothes are fine. Warm clothing should be provided for colder days. Children will go outside for a play period every day that the weather allows. When school is canceled at the city's public schools, preschool will also be canceled.

Parent-Teacher Conferences

Parent-teacher conferences will be held in October and in April. All parents are strongly encouraged to sign up for a parent-teacher conference. This is one way to keep open communication between parents and preschool staff. Written notes will be sent home with children once a week to keep parents informed on children's behavior and progress. Telephone calls will be made to parents in the event of particular concerns.

Other Items to Include in the Parent Handbook

The parent handbook should offer as much information as possible. If there are any supplies children need to bring, list them in the handbook. Other bits of information might be a policy about children bringing items from home, parking rules, class-party procedures, and a policy on birthday celebrations.

Curriculum

Curriculum should be described briefly in the parent handbook. If there is a published curriculum being used, it will need to be named. Any religious education within the curriculum will need to be made clear so that families know what their children will be taught while at the weekday ministry.

Staff

Staff people should be named, and their credentials noted. It is important for the handbook to provide information on how to contact the staff. Telephone numbers and e-mail addresses are appropriate.

Calendar for the Year

The most helpful parent handbooks include a calendar for the year. Vacation days, party days, and celebrations are all noted on the calendar. Providing a calendar in the handbook makes it easy for parents to keep all the information about the weekday ministry in one place. It will be a tool they can refer to throughout the year.

What to Include in the Employee Handbook

The format of the employee handbook will depend a great deal on the size of the weekday ministry and its staff. If the program employs only

List the items you currently include in your parent handbook.

What items do you need to add to the parent handbook?

List the items that you currently keep in each employee file.

one or two people, the written job description may be all that is needed. For larger programs, the employee handbook will serve as the place for employees to have access to policies and practices that will help them in their day-to-day activities on the job. Items that might be included in the employee handbook are as follows.

Definitions of Employee Status

The handbook will need to include definitions for each possible status for an employee. How is "full-time" defined? How is "part-time" defined? Other categories might be "Volunteer," "Teaching Assistant," "Temporary," "Substitute," or "New Employee on Probation." Some programs have another status of "probation" for staff members who have not met job expectations and are serving a "probationary period" after which further evaluation will be done to determine if they will remain on staff or be terminated. All of these terms should be defined in the employee handbook.

Quality Childcare Status

A statement about the quality of childcare or education that is offered by the weekday ministry would be appropriate to include in the employee handbook. For example, is the program licensed by the state? Is the program accredited by the National Association for the Education of Young Children or another organization? These qualifications should be noted.

What are the items you may need to consider adding to employee files?

Personnel Expectations

Significant space in the handbook will probably be devoted to personnel expectations. It needs to be noted if all members of the staff are required to have a child-abuse or criminal-background check, a health record, and a physical examination. What kind of in-service training or continuing education is expected each year?

The employee handbook is the place to list items that will be kept in each personnel file. The Gertrude Rummel Butler Child Development Center of the First United Methodist Church in Little Rock, Arkansas, lists the following items that are kept in each employee file:

- Basic information
- Education and training
- Health record
- Employment record and contact documentation
- Attendance record
- Date of employment
- Documented training and continuing education
- Authorization for release of confidential information contained in the state's child abuse and neglect registry
- Request for criminal record check
- Employee performance evaluation tools
- Completed W-4 form
- Completed I–9 form
- Signed statements that the staff member has:
    - read the handbook
    - reviewed licensing requirements
    - acknowledged the alcohol and other drugs abuse policy
    - attended orientation
    - been instructed in the use of a fire extinguisher

Determination of Salary

Include in the employee handbook salary scales, equations for determining salaries, and scheduled pay raises.

Employee Benefits

All employee benefits should be stated in the employee handbook. Possible benefits include medical health insurance, pension plan, vacation days, personal days, holidays, sick leave, unpaid leave of absence, employee childcare services, specified parking for staff, meals that are provided for staff, and continuing education opportunities. Many weekday ministries will not be financially secure enough to provide extensive benefits. However, even seemingly small benefits such as a birthday vacation day or an annual employee-appreciation dinner are ways to encourage the staff of the weekday ministry.

Employee Policies and Procedures

The employee handbook is the place to print all policies and procedures that apply to weekday-ministry staff. Below is a list of policies that every weekday ministry will want to establish. They are applicable to every setting where children are involved.

- Sexual Harassment Policy
- Disciplinary Policy
- Inclement Weather Policy
- Reporting Accidents That Have Occurred to Employees
- Reporting Accidents That Have Occurred to Children
- Recording/Reporting Absenteeism of Children
- Emergency Drills
- Use of Facilities
- Alcohol and Drug Abuse Policy
- Smoking Policy
- Safety Procedures
- Continuing Education Policy

Other policies and procedures that might be considered are:
- Family and Medical Leave Policy
- Absentee Policy
- Tardiness Policy
- Length of Work Week, Payroll Schedule, Clocking in and Out
- Staff Meetings and Communication
- Personal Phone Calls
- Solicitation of Parents
- Dress Code for Employees

Policies and Procedures for Working With Children

The employee handbook also needs to contain all policies and procedures that relate to working with children. These will differ from situation to situation, but generally they will include:
- Daily Communication With Parents
- Guideline to Speech and Actions (what is acceptable and what is not)
- Health, Safety, and Management of Classroom
- Diapering Procedure

What policies will need to be in place for your weekday-ministry employees?

69

- Disciplining of Children
- Sleeping Arrangements
- Nutritional Guidelines
- Playground Policies
- Fire and Tornado Drills
- Sick-Child Care Policy
- Medication Policy
- Authorization of People to Pick Up Children

What to Include in the Operations Manual for the Board of Directors

The operations manual for the board of directors can be a three-ring notebook that includes a copy of the articles of incorporation and bylaws for the weekday ministry, a copy of the parent handbook, a copy of the employee handbook, a place for notes, a place to keep copies of the minutes from board meetings, names and contact information for board members, and pages designed to describe the duties and responsibilities of the board of directors. These pages will include the following information:
- Schedule of Board Meetings
- Expectation of Attendance
- Description of the Responsibilities of the Board of Directors
- Description of the Duties of Each Board Officer
- Policy for the Dismissal of a Board Member
- Policy Regarding Length of Term for Board Members

Brochures About the Weekday Ministry

A weekday-ministry brochure is a way to describe the program. A purpose statement is essential as well as a brief list of services. If the weekday ministry has a mission statement, the brochure is an excellent place to state it. For example, "Where Children Grow in Spirit and Truth" or "A Caring Place for All God's Children" is a statement that might catch a person's attention. Specific information about hours of operation, location, and who to contact for more information also need to be part of the content of a brochure.

Brochures are both a source of information and a publicity tool. A brochure can highlight the program, spark interest, and be easily distributed. A brochure could be placed in a church bulletin or newsletter. It can be posted on a bulletin board or distributed as part of a "welcome basket" to new families in the community.

Brochure Appeal

Brochures should be appealing. They should be easy to read. Captions and colors can be used to separate sections of information. Colors should be used in a tasteful way. A brochure should be neither too dull nor too busy in appearance. The information needs to be well-organized, making it easy for a person to gain information about the weekday ministry at a glance. Photographs can be a powerful way to communicate activities and the atmosphere of a program. They show people in action, involved in the services that are provided. When using photographs, be sure to get written permission from anyone who appears in the photograph. For people under the age of eighteen you will need written permission from a parent or legal guardian.

Brochures come in many styles. A fold-out style is a compact way to package information. Another popular style for weekday-ministry brochures is the use of flip-up pages. Pages are layered on a sturdy base so that people can glance at the headings at the bottom of each page and know what information will be found on that page. They can then easily flip to the page of interest. Often, each page is a different color of paper, creating a rainbow appearance on the outside, with easy identification of individual topics.

Graphics are another tool that can help people identify sections of information. A graphic of a clock, for example, can head the daily schedule. A graphic of a glass of milk and an apple can accompany a block of text that describes the meals or snacks that the program provides.

The parent handbook, an employee handbook, an operations manual for the board of directors, and a program brochure are all tools that will help define the weekday ministry and make the day-to-day operations run much more smoothly.

What brochures do you currently use in your weekday program? When did you last update them?

Chapter Nine
ENROLLMENT

Enrollment requires marketing the weekday ministry, educating the community about the ministry, and recruiting participants for the ministry.

Marketing the Weekday Ministry

There are numerous ways to market any program the church may offer. Most likely, funding will not be available for an elaborate marketing campaign, so marketing of the weekday ministry will need to be kept simple, yet effective. Effective marketing will distribute information about the weekday ministry to the people who would benefit most from it.

Within the congregation, the weekday ministry can be advertised in the church newsletter, in the bulletin, and from the pulpit. Hopefully, throughout the planning and developing stages of the weekday ministry, the congregation will have been kept informed and involved, so that when it is time for enrollment, they will share in the excitement of the moment.

Beyond the walls of the church, the weekday ministry can be marketed with the use of brochures distributed in the neighborhood. Letters can be sent out to Sunday school families. A newspaper advertisement is another avenue for publicizing the program. A simple ad that gives a brief description of the services offered and provides information about whom to contact will suffice.

Registration

Registration provides the first list of who will participate in the weekday ministry. Whatever form registration takes, the goal is to develop a list of participants. Keep the registration form simple, as more detailed information can be gathered at enrollment. Registration allows people to get their children's names and birth dates on a list so that a place will be reserved for them in the program. From there, the appropriate forms can be distributed for enrollment.

The process of registration can begin with a letter of invitation and a registration form sent home with Sunday school children. This step can be extended to a nearby elementary school or the surrounding neighborhood. Phone calls from people whose interest is sparked by a brochure, a newspaper ad, or a banner displayed outside the church will begin to come into the church, and the same letter and form can be sent to them.

The Enrollment Packet

The enrollment packet contains everything necessary for a family to enroll their children in the weekday ministry. Often, the enrollment packet is sent out in early summer for children enrolling in a program that starts at the beginning of the school year. Sending them out too early may result in people misplacing them. Sending them out too late will rush families to fill out forms and get medical examinations completed. Year-long programs may send out enrollment packets to families on a waiting list as openings occur.

Licensing agencies usually send out a packet of forms to be copied and used for enrollment. When forms are provided by the state, they should be used for enrollment. If a particular form is not provided, one can be made to serve the purpose. Enrollment packets usually include the following: a cover letter, the parent handbook, required state forms, an enrollment form, and information about an enrollment open house or home visit. Many programs also send out a field-trip permission form, a photograph release form, a class-party sign-up sheet, and a field-trip assistance sheet.

The Cover Letter

The cover letter should be brief, stating what is included in the packet and any specific instructions families may need in completing enrollment. Each state has a list of child information that centers are required to keep on file. Know this list and use it as you put together your enrollment packet.

Child Information Form

A child information form is helpful for filling in any areas left out of the state forms. On a child information form you may ask parents to give information about their child's development, family background, child's interests, concerns about their child, and expectations they have about the weekday ministry.

Confidentiality

Any information you receive about a child or a child's family must be kept confidential. The information is given so that the weekday-ministry staff can better minister to the needs of that child and family. Only with a written agreement from the parents should any information be discussed with another person or agency. In case of suspicion of child abuse or neglect, this concern should be discussed only with the proper social agency in your area. In fact, it is the law that, as a childcare provider, you are required to report evidence of child abuse or neglect. This is not only a legal obligation, but a moral one as well.

What items do you include in your enrollment packet?

Enrollment Open House

Many weekday ministries that are structured for a particular time of year, such as the school year, open each new year with an enrollment open house. The open house is an invitation to families of the children who will be participants to come to the program room, turn in completed paperwork, pay fees and tuition, and ask questions. An open house can help children feel more comfortable when they arrive on the first day of the program.

For weekday ministries that operate year-round, a specific day for an open house might be replaced with individual invitations to new participants to come by and see the facilities. A childcare program, for example, might invite newly enrolled children and their families to come visit the center sometime before the first day that the children arrive for care. This type of visit can help relax both children and parents.

The Home Visit

A home visit can be a valuable enrollment practice. When the teacher or care provider visits children in their homes, the children feel important and the provider benefits from seeing children in their own environment. The relationships at home can be observed as well as the culture.

During a home visit many of the same things that would take place during an enrollment open house can happen. Completed forms can be turned in, fees and tuition can be paid, questions and concerns can be discussed. Children can meet their teacher or care provider—and they can show off their rooms, which they could not do at an open house.

A home visit may also be used as a time to do some preliminary assessment of children's developmental levels. The visitor may want to "play a few games" with the child. The games can include skills such as matching, sorting, fine or gross motor coordination, or listening to a short story. Children might be asked to "draw a picture of a person" or the home visitor could administer part of the Denver II developmental assessment. A Denver II form can be obtained from your local physician. The idea is to gather information which can be compared to future work and development in order to measure children's growth.

Enrollment Files

There are two files that need to be kept for each child in most weekday ministries. One is the official file and the other is a mobile file which can easily be carried on field trips or in emergency situations.

The mobile file is a folder for each child and staff person that should include: (1) emergency telephone numbers; (2) parental permission slips; (3) parental consent for emergency medical treatment; and (4) the child's health form.

The official file is kept at the center. There should be a file folder for each child and staff person that contains copies of everything in the mobile file. Additional forms include: (1) enrollment information; (2) assessment documentation; (3) accident forms that document any accident or illness a child has experienced while at the center; (4) copies of all communications with parents; (5) documentation of any troubling behavior.

Accident forms are usually provided by the state licensing agency. Keep these on hand. All accidents and illnesses need to be documented with an accident form.

Copies of communications with parents and documentation of troubling behavior are important to keep on file. These items will be helpful in the event of misunderstandings between staff and parents. Documentation of troubling behavior can help staff identify any triggers that might be related to a particular behavior. It may also help staff identify signs of child abuse, neglect, or undiagnosed illness or disorder with which a child may be dealing.

Access to Files

Files are to be kept confidential. Children's files are kept for the safety of the children and for the benefit of the staff as they seek to minister most effectively. They should be accessible only to the director and the teacher or childcare provider. Files should be kept in a locked cabinet. They are not to be accessible to members of the board of directors, church staff, the congregation, or parents of other children. Parents should be allowed to view the contents of their own child's file. Most of these documents will have been provided by the parent in the first place. If the contents of a child's file are asked for by a physician, therapist, counselor, social worker, or the child's school, the parent will need to sign a written consent form allowing the contents of the file to be shared. Also, if the care provider or director is going to tell another professional about the contents of the file, the parent must sign a consent form.

Payment of Fees and Tuition

A schedule of payment of fees and tuition should be included in the parent handbook and presented to families at the time of registration. Records need to be kept for all payments. Payments can be recorded in a record book, as well as by keeping a carbon copy of receipts for parents. This way there are at least two records of all payments. Periodic statements sent to parents of all payments they have made is helpful for families who are eligible to deduct the expense of the weekday ministry from their income tax or who want them for their own record keeping.

The process of marketing the weekday ministry, registration, and enrollment is important for the success of the program. As people hear about the ministry and are entered into it in an efficient, caring way, they will be more receptive to that which the weekday ministry has been designed to do.

Mission Valley United Methodist Church
123 Fourth Street
City, State 98765

Dear Parents,

This letter is to inform you of an exciting ministry that will be taking place at Mission Valley United Methodist Church. The Mission Valley Preschool will open on September 4th. It is designed for children ages three to five. Classes will be held weekday mornings from 9:00 A.M. to 11:30 A.M. Children who are one year away from kindergarten are encouraged to register for the Monday, Wednesday, Friday class. Children who are two years away from Kindergarten will benefit from the Tuesday/Thursday class.

Kathy Bryant is the preschool director and head teacher. Kathy has a degree in elementary education with twelve additional hours in early childhood education. She comes to us having taught preschool at the Sunshine Community Center for six years. Kathy is a bright, energetic woman who is concerned for the needs of young children. She is a member of the National Association for the Education of Young Children and Mission Valley United Methodist Church.

Assisting Kathy is Nancy Hogeland. Nancy is the mother of three children and has taught Sunday school for nine years. Kathy and Nancy make a great team.

The purpose of the Mission Valley Preschool is to provide an informal learning atmosphere in which children will grow physically, mentally, socially, and emotionally in order to develop a positive self-image and become prepared for the transition into kindergarten. The preschool is set in a Christian environment where God will be spoken of freely and the love of God demonstrated by the staff.

If you would like more information about Mission Valley Preschool, please call Kathy Bryant at XXX-XXXX. To register, fill out the form enclosed and send it to, or drop it by, the church office by August 1st.

Blessings,
Mission Valley Preschool
Board of Directors
David Mossman, chair

SAMPLE REGISTRATION FORM
Mission Valley United Methodist Church Preschool

Name of child: _____

Date of birth: _____

Name of parent or guardian: _____

Home address: _____

Home telephone: _____ E-mail: _____

Father's work phone: _____ Mother's work phone: _____

If your child goes to daycare, who is the daycare provider? _____

_____

Check which session you wish to register your child for:

For children who are one year away from kindergarten:

___ Monday   ___ Wednesday   ___ Friday

For children who are two years away from kindergarten:

___ Tuesday   ___ Thursday

Send this form to: Kathy Bryant, Mission Valley United Methodist Church, 123 Fourth Street, City, State 98765 by August 1st.

Once we receive this registration form, you will be sent an enrollment packet. If you have any questions, call Kathy Bryant at XXX-XXXX.

Mission Valley United Methodist Church
123 Fourth Street
City, State 98765
XXX-XXXX
Chris Von Felt, Pastor

Dear Parents,

Your child is registered to enroll at the Mission Valley Preschool for the coming school year. Enclosed you will find all forms necessary for completing the enrollment process. They include

- Child Information Sheet

- Emergency Form

- Medical Report (includes immunization record)

- Medical Examination Form
  (To be filled out by a physician or registered nurse)

- Parental Consent for Emergency Medical Care

- Photo Permission Slip

- Walking Field Trip Permission Slip

- Parent Handbook

- Permission for Water Activities

Bring the completed forms to the preschool room at Mission Valley United Methodist Church sometime between 9 A.M. and 12 P.M. or 5 P.M. and 7 P.M. on August 20th.

At that time we can go over the forms together and you may pay the enrollment fee and first month's tuition. Your child will have a chance to meet the teachers and explore the preschool room. The whole process should take between 15 and 30 minutes.

If you are unable to come on August 20th, please contact me to make other arrangements. Feel free to call me at either the church or my home (YYY-YYYY).

Sincerely,
Kathy Bryant, Preschool Director

SAMPLE CHILD INFORMATION FORM
Mission Valley Preschool

Name of Child: _____ Date of Birth: _____

Family Background
Names and ages of brothers and sisters: _____

_____

Child's parents or guardian (circle one)
married   divorced   separated   remarried   never married

Additional helpful information about child's family setting: _____

_____

Was there anything unusual about your child's birth? _____

_____

Is your child adopted? _____

    How old was your child when he or she was adopted? _____

    Does your child know that she or he was adopted? _____

Child's Development
At what age did your child start to walk? _____

At what age was your child toilet-trained? _____

Can you understand most of what your child says? _____

What toys does your child like to play with? _____

Has your child spent short periods of time away from you (daycare, preschool, Sunday school, church nursery, play group)? _____

_____

Do you have books or magazines at home that your child enjoys? _____

_____

Do you have any concerns about your child's development? _____

Does your child have any illnesses or disorders that we should know about? _____

What do you expect your child to gain from the Mission Valley Preschool experience?

_____

SAMPLE PREREGISTRATION FORM
Children's Activity Program (CAP)
An Afterschool Program for Children in Grades 1-6

Child's Name: _____

Grade and School: _____

Address Where Child Resides: _____

Others in Child's Household: _____

Name of Legal Guardian: _____

Relationship to Child: _____

Home Address: _____

Home Phone: _____

E-mail: _____

Place of Employment: _____

Work Phone: _____

Cell Phone: _____

Name of a Second Contact Person: _____

Relationship to Child: _____

Home Address: _____

Home Phone: _____

Place of Employment: _____

Work Phone: _____

Cell Phone: _____

How will your child be arriving at CAP?
- ❑ School Bus
- ❑ Private Drop Off (By whom?) _____
- ❑ Walking
- ❑ Other (Explain) _____

List people who have permission to pick your child up from CAP.

Name	Relationship to Child	Phone Number
_____	_____	_____
_____	_____	_____
_____	_____	_____
_____	_____	_____

At what time will your child be picked up? _____

Emergency Contacts

    Child's Doctor: _____

    Hospital Preference: _____

    Others: _____

Is there a parental separation or divorce custody situation of which the CAP staff should be aware? If yes, please explain. _____

_____

Who will be responsible for payment of CAP fees?
If different from the legal guardian, complete the following information:

    Name: _____

    Address: _____

    Home Phone: _____

    Work Phone: _____

Does your child have any allergies? _____

_____

Does your child take medication? If yes, please state the name and the dosage.

_____

Will medication need to be given during CAP hours? _____

Does your child have any chronic illness or disorder? _____

Please note any information or concerns you have that might be helpful to CAP staff.

_____

_____

Chapter Ten
THE PROGRAM SPACE

WEEKDAY MINISTRIES

The Importance of Space

Space is an important part of a weekday ministry. Space can make the difference between a pleasant experience and a stressful experience for staff and children. The atmosphere of the program space communicates a mood. Space can be inviting or cold and unfriendly.

The way colors are incorporated into the space says much about the character and mood of the whole program. A space that is dirty and dark, for example, offers a different feel than would a space decorated in bright colors and a variety of textures. A nursery painted in pastels with an attractive border around the walls seems much more inviting to infants and their parents than would an outdated wooden crib stuck in a damp corner of a church basement.

The atmosphere should communicate something about the goal of the weekday ministry through the media of walls and floors, lighting and air temperature, fixtures and furniture, toys and materials. The program space serves as a reflection of what takes place within that space. It should communicate who the space is designed for and what type of activities take place there. Simply by looking at the space used for a weekday ministry's daycare, a person should immediately know that the area is designed for small children and for children's safety, comfort, and development.

Developmentally Appropriate Space

Like every other element in the weekday ministry, space should be developmentally appropriate for those being served. The size of the furniture and equipment should comfortably fit the size of the people using the space. Chairs should be made at a height so that children can easily sit down in them and stand back up without having to hop on and off. Tables need to be in proportion to the chairs. All items that are there for the enjoyment of the children need to be shelved at a level that makes them accessible. Toilet facilities that are sized to young children make self-help skills much easier for children to master. If the facility does not have a toilet or sink built at a child's level, safe steps can be provided. Make sure that the steps are stable and durable. Unstable steps are a safety hazard.

Toys and supplies need to be appropriate for the developmental levels represented by the children in the program. Not all children, even those in the same age group, will be at the same developmental stage. Therefore toys and supplies need to be available representing a range of skill levels—puzzles of varying difficulty or a variety of manipulatives requiring different muscle groups, for example.

There should be toys to help children develop in all areas stated in the goals and objectives. Here is a list of some sample toys and equipment. The list is by no means exhaustive.

Motor Development
- Crayons, pencils, markers
- Scissors
- Puzzles
- Manipulatives
- Construction paper
- Writing paper
- Drawing paper
- Collage materials
- Non-toxic glue and paste
- Paintbrushes
- Paints
- Play dough
- Balls
- Balance beam
- Climbing equipment
- Tricycles, scooters
- Hoops
- Digging area
- Digging toys
- Crawl-through equipment
- Bean-bag toss
- Blocks

Social Development
- Dramatic play center
- Puppets
- Dolls, doll house
- Felt story board
- Play kitchen, dishes, food
- Dress-up clothes, hats, shoes
- Mirror

- Toy cash register and money
- Play telephones

Cognitive Development
- Puzzles
- Counting games
- Matching games
- Sorting games
- Books
- Tape or compact-disc player
- Appropriate children's music
- Rhythm instruments
- Magnifying glass
- Magnets
- Measuring and pouring equipment

Spiritual Development
- Age-appropriate "Bibles" and Bible stories
- Altar table—child-size
- Christian symbols and pictures
- Bible verses

Just as all children are not in the same place developmentally, neither are all children in the same place culturally or experientially. The program space should affirm such variety. Pictures on the wall, bulletin boards, displays, and books can be used to depict the differences and similarities that exist among the participants of the weekday ministry. A room decorated with elements of human diversity will make more people feel welcome.

Indoor Space

Every state will have requirements for indoor space. This information will be found in the licensing packet. Always plan according to the state licensing information. Never assume that what is required in one state is the same in the next. Indoor space requirements may range from 30 to 35 square feet per child.

State Fire-Safety Codes

The state fire marshal will also have indoor space requirements. Usually these have to do with the number of exits needed for each room used by the weekday ministry, the type of electrical outlets, fire-extinguisher upkeep, and fire-alarm systems. For many churches starting a weekday ministry, the largest initial expense is in bringing the church building up to state fire-safety codes. Check with the state fire marshal early in the planning stages. Sometimes churches have had to delay the opening of a weekday ministry until they made necessary changes in order to meet fire-safety codes. This delay is a disappointment to everyone involved.

Annual Health Inspection

The licensing agency requires a health inspection of the facilities annually. Often, this is conducted by the county health nurse. Here is a list of some of the things that will be observed during the annual inspection.

What toys and equipment do you have available in each of the following areas?

Fine Motor Development

Gross Motor Development

Social Development & Dramatic Play

Cognitive Development

Emergent Literacy

Music and Movement

Spiritual Development

Science and Exploration

The list is not exhaustive, simply a starting place as you evaluate the program space.

Windows and Doors
❑ Are the windows and doors properly installed and easy to open in the case of an emergency?
❑ Are windows set high enough in the wall that a child cannot accidentally run through them?
❑ Are exits properly marked?
❑ Does each window have a screen on it?

Floors
❑ Are the floors clean and safe for children to play on?
❑ Is carpet in good repair? Are floors without cracks?

Lighting
Some states require a specified amount of light to be present in the room.
❑ Is the indoor space well-lit?
❑ Do sleeping areas have enough light to allow for freedom of movement?

Food Preparation Area
❑ Are food preparation areas clean and clear of toxic hazards?
❑ Is refrigeration available?
❑ Is garbage placed in a covered container?
❑ Are eating utensils kept clean?

Diapering Area
❑ Is there one area designated for diapering?
❑ Are all necessary supplies stored in that area?
❑ Is there a lined receptacle for disposable diapers and wipes?
❑ Is a hand-washing area nearby?

Electrical Concerns
❑ Are all electrical outlets covered?
❑ Are there any extension cords that will need to be removed?

Temperature Control
❑ Is the space heated, ventilated, and cooled to the comfort of the children? Some states require that the temperature of each room shall not be less than 65 degrees Fahrenheit or more than 90 degrees Fahrenheit.

Poisons
❑ Are all medicines, household poisons, and other dangerous substances and instruments in locked storage?

Pets
❑ Are there any animals that would represent a hazard to children on the premises?
❑ Is the pet area maintained in a sanitary manner and away from food-preparation areas?
❑ Do any dogs or cats have current immunizations as recommended by a veterinarian?
❑ Is the immunization record on file in the facility?

Posted Information

❑ Is there a fire-escape plan posted in each room?

❑ Is the discipline policy posted where parents can easily see it?

❑ Is there a record of fire and tornado drills posted?

Other Space Requirements

A working telephone must be on the premises with a list of emergency numbers posted next to it. In addition to numbers for the fire department, ambulance, and doctor, it can be helpful to have a list of parent and guardian phone numbers near the phone.

There will also need to be storage space for supplies and equipment. Some things can be kept accessible on a shelf at all times. Other items will need a place to be stored that is out of sight and inaccessible. Children will need a place to store their personal belongings. Hooks for coats and a cubby or box for each child need to be available.

If children sleep during weekday-ministry hours, there should be a designated sleep space. This may be the same space that is used for another activity during the day, but at a certain time it becomes the sleep space. That is the only place where children sleep.

Arranging Indoor Space

When considering the arrangement of indoor space there are a few things to keep in mind. If the weekday ministry will be serving different age groups, space may need to be divided according to the needs of each age group. For example, infants will need space for cribs, while preschoolers will need some gross motor equipment, and school-aged children may need larger-sized tables and chairs. Take into account the areas that will be needed during a day.

- Food preparation area
- Eating area
- Craft/art/writing area
- Sleep area
- Toileting/diapering area
- Quiet area for reading
- Circle-time area
- Area for indoor games
- Dramatic play area
- Block area
- Gross motor area
- Homework area

Often, the necessary areas are labeled "centers," as they are centers of certain activities. As centers are arranged in the space, keep in mind the flow of movement. Good planning would not have children with dripping paintings stepping over children in the block center in order to hang a painting to dry or to wash up. Which centers need to be in close proximity to a sink? a corner? a wall?

An effective space arrangement can reduce discipline problems. Ask any parent of young children what children will do in an open space, and the answer will be, "They run." Arrange centers in ways that avoid large

What areas will be needed in your weekday-ministry program?

open spaces or long aisles. Determine how many children can productively play in each center and provide only that number of chairs, carpet squares, or stickers on the floor. That way children can easily see when a center is full and when they will need to find another activity.

At the end of this chapter are a couple of room arrangements. Have fun exploring the indoor space available and designing your space for an effective ministry.

Outdoor Space

Each state has outdoor space requirements as well as indoor. Again, the required space is not the same in every state. For example, Texas requires 80 square feet of outdoor play space for each child using the area at one time. Alabama requires at least 60 square feet of outdoor play area for each child, and Kansas falls in the middle, requiring 75 square feet of outdoor play space for each child using the space at any given time.

Safety

Outdoor play space should be fenced in and supervised whenever children are using the area. Children should be easily viewable when on equipment, even in crawl spaces. Ideally, the outdoor play area should provide places of both sunshine and shade. The space should be free of hazardous conditions. These can include everything from broken branches on the ground to rusty nails or protruding corners on equipment. Equipment will need to be maintained so that there are no broken parts, missing parts, protruding bolts, rust, splinters, cracks, or holes which might injure a child. Pay attention to noticeable gaps that might cause head entrapments. The board of directors or church trustees will need to schedule an annual playground inspection so that space and equipment will be kept in good repair.

Another safety element to take into consideration is the fall surfacing. The ground under equipment, including a six-foot fall zone around equipment, should provide a soft, shock-absorbent surface. The depth of the surface needed to avoid serious injury will depend upon the height of the equipment. Sand, mulch, or shock-absorbent tiles are preferable under

U.S. Consumer Product Safety Commission Necessary depth for loose-fill surfacing materials	
Height of equipment and type and minimum uncompressed depth of material at point of impact:	
5 feet	6 inches of fine sand, coarse sand, or pea gravel
6 feet	6 inches of double-shredded bark mulch, engineered wood fibers, or pea gravel
7 feet	6 inches of wood chips or 9 inches of engineered wood fibers or pea gravel
9 feet	12 inches of fine sand
10 feet	9 inches of wood chips or double-shredded bark mulch or 12 inches of pea gravel
11 feet	12 inches of wood chips or double-shredded bark mulch

Source: "Handbook for Public Playground Safety," by the U.S. Consumer Product Safety Commission, page 5 (www.cpsc.gov/cpscpub/pubs/playpubs.html).

equipment. Gravel, grass, or concrete can result in child injuries. The chart lists the minimum depths necessary, but in fact the Product Safety Commission recommends that at least twelve inches of any surface-fill material be used.

Equipment should be sturdy and properly anchored in the ground. Sandboxes need to be kept clean of debris and animal feces. It is most advisable that sand boxes be covered when not in use.

Developmentally Appropriate

Like all other aspects of the curriculum, the outdoor play space should consist of developmentally appropriate equipment and activities. Some possible equipment for children two to five years of age would be: activity panels, small slides, lower platforms from which children can jump, spring rocking equipment, sand/water table, crawl tunnels, and play houses. Balls, hoops, bubbles, and tossing games are also appropriate. For children ages five to twelve, appropriate equipment includes: swings, horizontal ladders, chain and net climbers, free-standing arch climbers, sliding poles, merry-go-rounds, and track gliders. Swings can be a wonderful means of developing gross motor skills; however, swings and seesaws require constant, close supervision at all times. Take this into consideration before installing swings, seesaws, merry-go-rounds, or tall slides. There may be alternatives that will also allow for gross motor development but are less dangerous for children.

The outdoor space should be an extension of the indoor curriculum. As you plan the outdoor space, keep in mind the goals of the weekday ministry. It should be fun, safe, and age appropriate.

Sharing Space

Most churches do not have space enough to allow each program or group that meets in the church to have an exclusive space. Shared space is an issue that needs to be dealt with. For example, a Sunday school class meets in the same space that the preschool occupies during the week. The church kitchen is used to prepare funeral dinners as well as meals and snacks for the daycare. The restrooms are used by the children who attend the afterschool program on weekdays and by the congregation on Sundays. The fellowship hall is used by the weekday ministry when weather does not permit children to go outside. It is also used for Sunday fellowship dinners, funeral dinners, wedding receptions, and the Wednesday night Bible study. How can shared space be managed to the satisfaction of all involved?

Space issues involve numerous people and groups in the church: the weekday-ministry staff, Sunday school teachers, the church custodian, the kitchen committee, the church office personnel, study groups, and others.

Shared space can sometimes make or break a weekday ministry. It can be a source of stress and conflict. Think about the following situations that churches have had to deal with.

Sunday school teachers arrive on Sunday morning to discover that the chalk board they use in their classroom has been moved to the preschool room. It has a list of program songs written on it with a message "Do Not Erase!"

The weekday-ministry staff arrive on Monday morning to discover that their supply of finger paint was used for Sunday school. Brushes have been left out, the sink is blue and orange, and paintings have been left to dry on top of the toddlers' activity tables.

The weekday-ministry assistant goes to the church kitchen to prepare lunch trays. The kitchen is filled with women who are preparing for a salad luncheon. The carrot sticks that were meant for the children's lunch trays have been added to a relish dish and served to another group.

When people file into the Sunday school classroom they discover that the Lenten altar table with its draped cross and crown of thorns has been transformed into a puppet stage by the weekday-ministry staff.

Each of these scenarios could cause upset, disagreement, and even resentment among people using the space and equipment. How could they be avoided or handled in a way that would prove beneficial and productive?

Facing Space Issues

Like people who share a household, people who share space in a church building rely upon communication and consideration to make things work. Maintaining them is the key to shared space. To accomplish this, it is necessary to plan periodic meetings of all people who are affected by shared space, shared scheduling, and shared personnel. A weekday-ministry representative needs to be a part of calendar planning sessions. All space needs to be reserved and noted in one location. The church office can be the place for each group to reserve space in the church on one large calendar. Even regularly scheduled events like fixing daycare lunches from 11:30 to 12:00 each morning should be noted on the calendar. Labels help people know which items are available to them and which items belong to another group. Designated and labeled storage areas, cabinets, and shelves save people from a lot of assumptions that all materials and equipment are there for the taking.

Written policies are a clear form of communication. Cleanup schedules for shared bathrooms leave no room for one group to assume that the cleanup is always up to someone else. A policy for the use of audio-visual equipment can clearly state that the equipment must be checked out through the church office and returned to its proper storage space after use. Therefore, no one will be engaged in a mad search for the VCR just before the Disciple Bible study meets on Monday night. Policies stating who pays for certain equipment, supplies, and utilities are useful. If the Sunday school and the weekday ministry use construction paper from the same supply cabinet, who pays for it? Perhaps a percentage can be worked out, depending on usage. This can be stated in a policy. Lists of things that need to be put away on Fridays or Sundays are helpful in preparing space for the next group to use.

Open communication between the people who are sharing space is essential. If the weekday ministry takes place in space that is used by a Sunday school class, you and the Sunday school teacher will need to check with each other often about concerns. Don't always wait until a concern has become a frustration. Ask the Sunday school teacher and superintendent if they have any concerns. Is there anything that the weekday-ministry staff might do to make the transition to Sunday morning easier?

Notes can be a form of open communication. Leave notes of appreciation or explanation to the other person who shares the space. For example, "We left our paintings on the shelf to dry. Feel free to move them to the top of the preschool cabinet if you need the shelf space." Or, "Thanks for cleaning out the sink so well. I could see myself in it!" Simple notes can help to build a cooperative working relationship.

Positive sharing of space requires both cooperation and respect. Respect church traditions and sacred spaces. If there is an altar table in the room that is used as a worship center during Sunday school, leave it as is no matter how tempting it is to use it as a puppet theater or a project display table.

Churches often have revered furnishings, paintings, or wall hangings. Some of the rooms or furnishings may have been dedicated in honor or memory of a person or group. Always check before removing an item from the room or wall. If the room has been named the Alice Myers Memorial Nursery, do not take down the plaque with that name. Simply tell people that the weekday ministry takes place in the Alice Myers Memorial Nursery. Respect church traditions. When an item is given to the weekday ministry as a memorial gift, always write a note of appreciation in the church newsletter and to the family of the person in whose memory it was given.

> Thank you for the playground equipment that was purchased with the gifts given in memory of your mother, Wilma Holbroock. The activity panels were installed last week and the children are enjoying them. They provide an opportunity for the children not only to develop their large muscles but also to practice some problem-solving skills. Through your gift, your mother's love for young children will continue to touch the lives of children for many years. Thank you.

Sharing space is an opportunity for education of both the children in the program and the congregation. The weekday-ministry staff may need to educate the congregation about how normal use of the facilities will cause some wear and tear. When children play on the carpet every weekday, the carpet will slowly deteriorate. Children touch glass doors and windows, leaving finger marks. Accepting this kind of wear on the facility is part of the mission of any church that offers a weekday ministry. Children need to be educated and taught to respect other people's property and the church. Just as we do not color on another child's paper, we do not scratch up the furniture or leave the room a mess.

Seek to make sharing space an opportunity to build positive relationships. Educate the congregation about the weekday program, and the children about respecting the church. (Many of these ideas, and several others, can be found in the pamphlet *Fifty Nifty Ideas for Improving Relationships Between Religious Congregations and Their Early Childhood Weekday Programs,* published by the Ecumenical Child Care Network.)

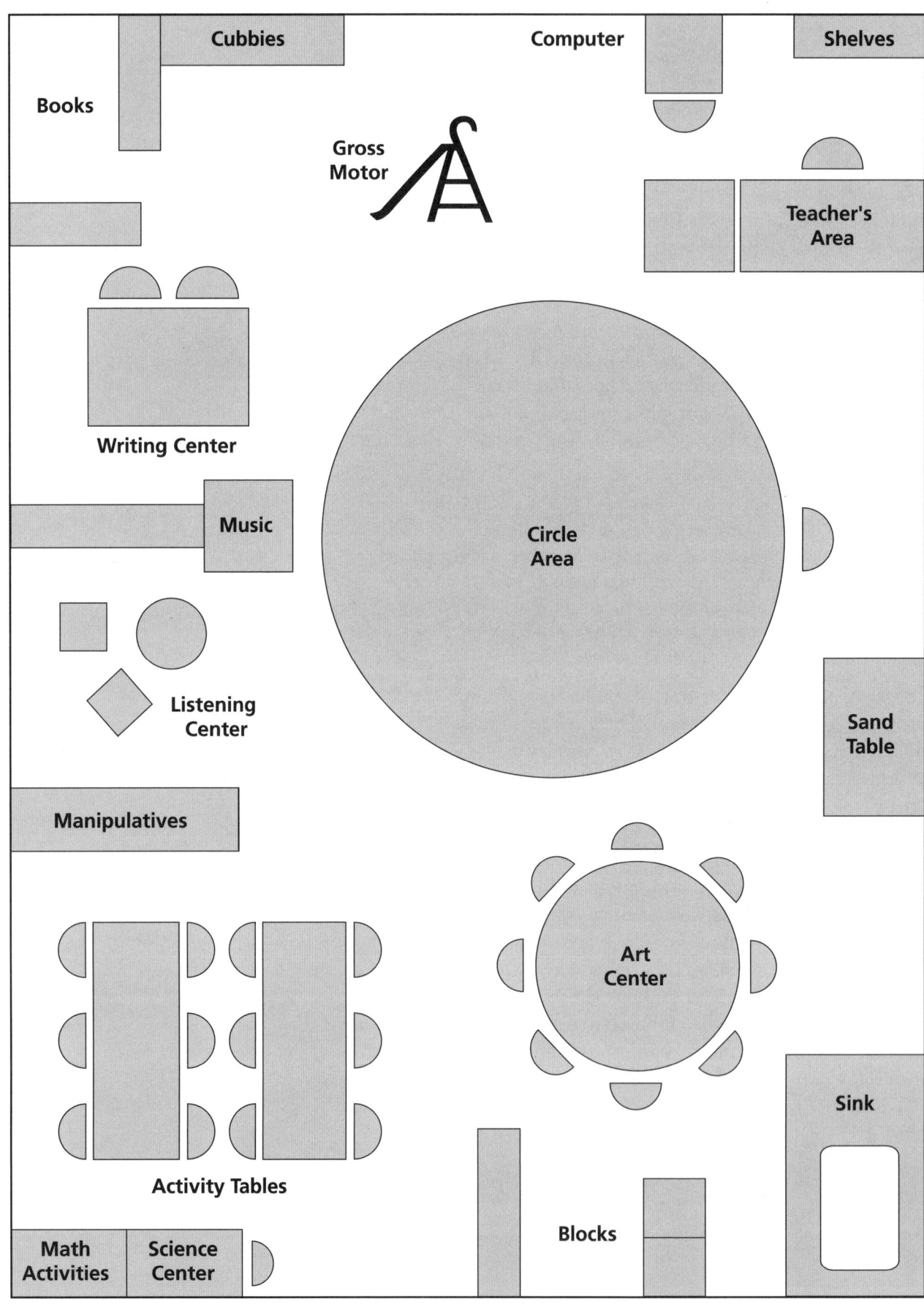

Cubbies

Computer

Shelves

Books

Gross Motor

Teacher's Area

Writing Center

Music

Circle Area

Listening Center

Sand Table

Manipulatives

Art Center

Sink

Activity Tables

Blocks

Math Activities

Science Center

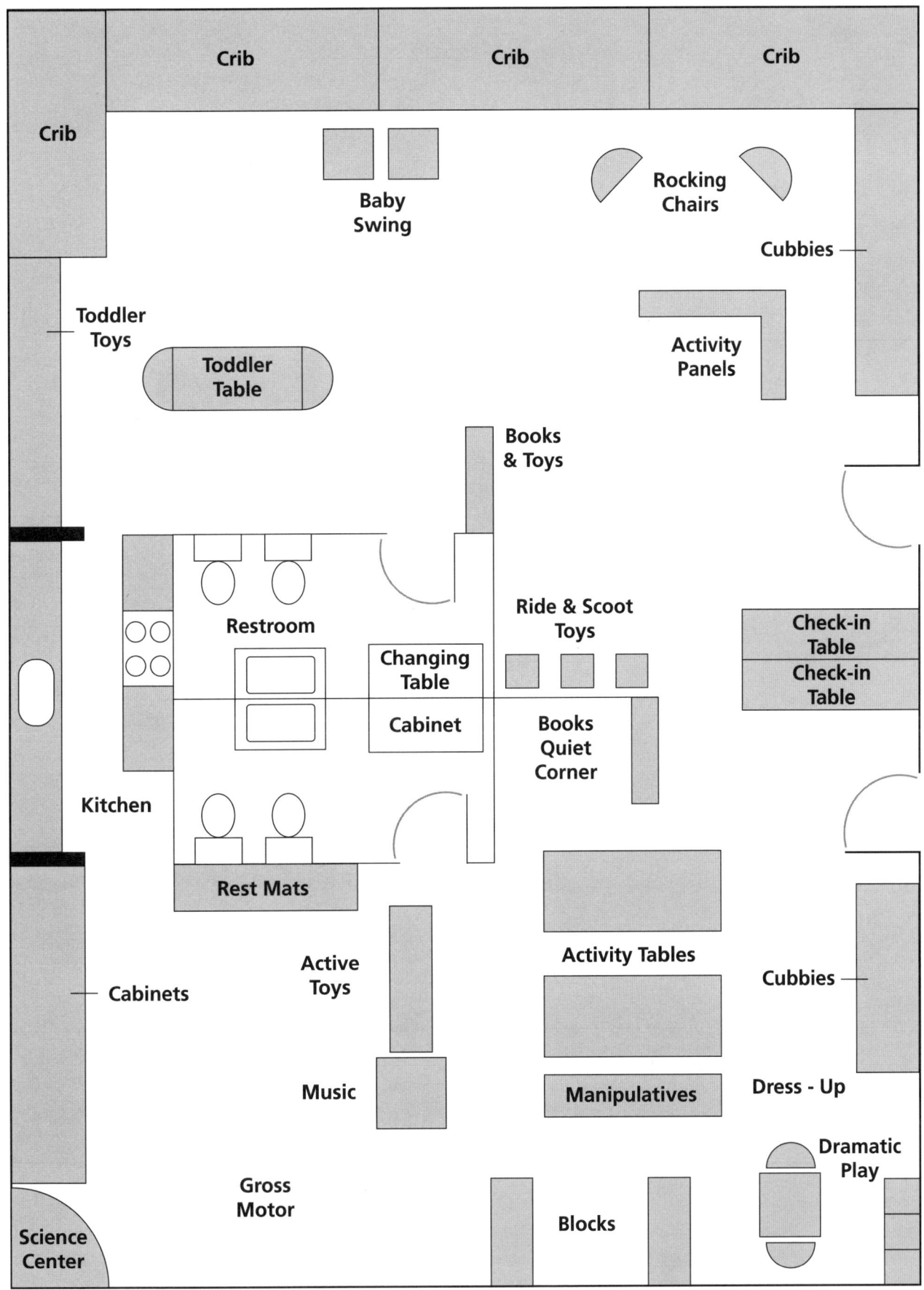

Chapter Eleven
Educating the Congregation and Community

Education may be one of the goals of the weekday ministry, whether through a preschool program, a daycare, an afterschool program, or a sick-child care program. The education required for a weekday ministry to be successful goes beyond the program itself. The congregation will need to be educated about the program. The community beyond the church will need to be educated about the church and the weekday ministry it offers. The program staff needs to learn from the church and community in order to meet the needs that lie before them.

Educating the Congregation About Program Goals

The first step in educating the congregation about the weekday ministry is to make it aware of the need for the program. The congregation needs to claim ownership of the program goals that are offered through the weekday ministry. The need for the program can be communicated in many ways. A director's column in the church newsletter can be used to present the needs in the church and community that the program goals seek to meet. Prayers for the children in the program and their families can be printed in the Sunday worship bulletin for people to take home and use as part of their devotional time during the week.

I pray, O God, for children whose parents cannot be home for them after school each day. They are restless, hungry, and need an outlet for their energy. Some of them face homework assignments and need assistance to complete them. May the caring hand of Jesus Christ touch these children through the afterschool program. Equip the staff with all that they need to care for these children, helping them know that they have a place where they belong after school. And if there be any thing I might do to assist in meeting their needs, make it clear to me in my heart and my mind. Amen.

Regular reports to the church council can be used as opportunities for educating the congregation. Make the report celebrative, even entertaining. Invite groups in the church to view the rooms used by the weekday ministry and see the projects that are taking place. Use photographs or videos of the ministry in action. The more the congregation is exposed to the weekday ministry, and the more they know about what happens there, the better they can tell others about it and claim it as part of their own ministry.

Share learning events that take place in the weekday ministry. Display projects where they can easily be viewed by members of the congregation. A weekday-ministry bulletin board can be a great way to display photographs or artwork. Invite the congregation to attend weekday-ministry programs. If a Christmas program is an annual event for the weekday ministry, encourage the congregation to enjoy it. If the weekday ministry has religious curriculum, encourage the worship committee to include the children from the weekday ministry in the worship service on occasion. They might sing a song, lead a litany, or dramatize a passage of Scripture, always depending on the developmental level of the children.

A Sense of Ownership

It is important for the congregation to share ownership in the weekday ministry. Shared ownership results in shared enthusiasm for and commitment to the program. Milestones in the life of the weekday ministry can be celebrated in the weekly worship service. These might include receiving a license to operate, important anniversaries for the daycare, the opening of each preschool year, preschool graduation, or the one-hundredth enrollment in the afterschool program. Mission moments that are related to the weekday ministry that takes place during the week can be shared during the Sunday morning worship service. Perhaps the children in the program could design the worship-bulletin cover for the Week of the Young Child in April.

Sharing Common Goals

The congregation and the weekday ministry need to share common goals for building updates, repairs, and decorating. The church should install a fire-alarm system, not just because it is required for the weekday ministry but because it is a safety device that might save the lives of everyone in the church. The carpeting and the walls need to be kept clean and attractive, not just for the weekday ministry but so the entire congregation can feel good about the appearance of their church. The outdoor play area can be developed for the benefit of all the children who participate in vacation Bible school, study groups, and childcare during meetings as well as the weekday ministry. Shared ownership includes shared goals, shared enthusiasm, and shared celebrations.

Continuing Education for the Congregation

There may be times when continuing-education events for the weekday-ministry staff can be extended to members of the congregation. Invite the congregation to participate in in-service training that could benefit them as well as the program staff. A first-aid or CPR class could benefit many members of the congregation. A seminar on helping children deal with grief would be beneficial to the weekday-ministry staff, the church staff, Sunday school teachers, and parents.

The church newsletter column could be used to teach about the importance of developmentally appropriate practice or brain research. The congregation can be invited to celebrate the Week of the Young Child by wearing ribbons made by the children in the weekday ministry or by taking up a collection to purchase supplies for the weekday program.

A Program for Church Groups

As director for the weekday ministry, make yourself available to talk with groups in the church about the weekday program or issues related to the children the program serves. United Methodist Women, United Methodist Men, United Methodist Youth Fellowship, and Sunday school classes are often looking for programs for their group.

Educating the Community About Program Goals

Marketing the weekday ministry can be a means of educating the community. Sharing the goals and the activities that are designed to meet those goals gives people a greater understanding of the important work that is taking place in the church. Brochures delivered to the local schools help inform parents and school professionals about the needs that are being met through the weekday ministry. Newspaper articles about upcoming or recent events in the program help to keep the happenings of the weekday ministry before the community. Remember, pictures tell a story. Pictures in brochures, newspapers, and newsletters or on bulletin boards will tell a story about the children who are involved in the weekday ministry.

Public Invitations

Just as the congregation can be invited to some in-service training events for program staff, sometimes an invitation to the general public offers them not only an educational experience but also an awareness of the weekday ministry and of the church. Parenting classes or parent discussion groups could be sponsored by the weekday ministry. A seminar on puppetry or a workshop on making activity travel bags for young children could be beneficial to many people in the larger community beyond the walls of the church. Through such extended outreach, new ministry will take place.

Educating Parents

An early childhood special-education teacher once stated that "ninety percent of early childhood education is parent education." Efforts made only during weekday-ministry hours will make a small difference in a child's life. When the ministry goals are extended to life at home, it will make a big difference in the life of a child. Parents need to understand what is developmentally appropriate for their children. When are they asking too much of their children and when are they not expecting enough?

In what ways might you educate the congregation about the weekday ministry?

What kind of nutrition do children require? Which behaviors are typical stages of development, and which behaviors warrant concern?

Papers and Progress Reports

Parents need to know what their children are experiencing while at the weekday ministry. Papers and projects sent home with notes can explain to parents what children have learned through the process and how that learning can continue at home. Progress reports are helpful in keeping parents informed of their child's progress. Reports can bring up concerns that the weekday-ministry staff may have and open up the communication process with the family. Progress reports can be lengthy checklists of a child's developmental progress or they can be simple forms that record a child's daily activities.

Take-Home Activities

Activities that children can take home and share with their families are another way to involve parents in the weekday ministry. Activities can be checked out, sent home, and returned for another child to check out. File-folder games are easy to make and handy to put into a child's bag to carry back and forth. Activities should be age-appropriate with any instructions written out in a way that is easily understood. Color games, shape games, letter games, number games, puzzles, sequencing cards, or simple card games all make fun take-home activities for small children.

A Weekday-Ministry Newsletter

A weekday-ministry newsletter can prompt parents to encourage learning at home. Include names of books that parents can read to children, activities that will help children develop small and large muscles, and games that will help children develop cognitive skills. Newsletters should be appealing to the eye. Use color, if it is available. Insert pictures of the children involved in activities. Parents will read about their children when they are mentioned by name or pictured. Make the newsletter easy to read. Short notes will be read more readily than lengthy articles. Make the newsletter fun.

Conferring With Parents

Parents need to be consulted about how their child is doing in the weekday ministry. Parent-teacher conferences are usually planned for preschool programs. Notes and phone calls can be used when a concern arises in any type of weekday ministry.

When conferring with parents, always share something positive about the child's progress. Even if things are not going well, think of something affirming about the child that you can share with the parent. Share concerns in a kind way, rather than with an accusing tone of voice. For example, which sounds better to a parent's ear?

—"Charlie spends most of the day in time-out for hitting and kicking the other children. If you can't teach him not to do this, he will have to be dismissed from the weekday ministry."

Or

—"Charlie loves to paint. I like his enthusiasm when we paint. He has, however, been expressing some aggressive feelings by hitting and kicking the other children. This is not appropriate. Is there anything you can think of that might be bothering Charlie? Let's think of a way to handle this behavior together, so that expectations at preschool and at home will be the same."

—"Sally is not keeping up with the other children. She does not know her colors yet, she will not sit still during a short story, and she refuses to lie quietly at rest time. I think you should talk to a doctor and find out what is wrong with her."

Or

—"Sally approaches life with such excitement. I can always count on her to try any new activity. I am concerned, however, that she may have some developmental delays. Colors are a problem for her, and her attention span is still short. If it is agreeable to you, I would like to have Sally screened. It can help us to identify areas where Sally may need help. If we can identify them early, Sally can benefit from the resources that are available."

Conclude the conference on a positive note. A simple statement like "Thank you for your cooperation" or "I'm sure we can work this out together" will leave parents feeling good about the parent-teacher relationship.

Learning From the Congregation

To lead an effective ministry within a church, there are many things that a weekday-ministry staff needs to learn from members of the congregation and the church itself. Become familiar with the structure of the church. Who takes care of administrative duties? Who do you go to when something needs to be repaired? Who handles the program calendar? Who makes the final decisions about the ministries that take place in the church? Visit with the pastor about his or her vision for ministry. Learn where the church has been in the past and how the church sees its role in the future.

Sacred Places

Every church has sacred times and places. Some of them are shared by most churches. The sanctuary is set apart for the purpose of worship. The baptismal font is used exclusively for baptisms. Sacred times may include the seasons of the church year, anniversaries of major events in the life of the church, or annual festivals that have become part of the church tradition. If the church has a tradition of serving a chicken noodle supper on the first day of hunting season, that needs to be respected as weekday-ministry plans are made that might involve the use of the kitchen or fellowship hall. Sacred places can be anything from a room to an altar table to a particular cabinet in the church kitchen. Learn what these are so that the weekday ministry's staff and participants can treat them with respect. Each church has a long history of events, losses, celebrations, gifts, and dedications that define how the space, time, appliances, and equipment are to be used.

Introduce Yourself to the Church

Whether you are new to the local congregation where you work or have been a lifelong member, you will need to introduce yourself to the church as the director of the weekday ministry. This is your opportunity to voice your enthusiasm for the program and your concerns related to the needs of the children you serve, their families, and the community. Write newsletter columns, share mission moments in worship, make regular reports about the weekday ministry to the administrative council, and visit often with the director of Christian education and the pastor about your vision for the program and how the church might help. Suggest ways that the weekday ministry might enhance the life of the church. The important thing is to be a visible presence in the life of the church.

Discover the Congregation

Discover the talents and experiences that exist in the congregation. The church is made up of individuals, each with a unique set of talents, gifts, interests, and experiences. Find out who these people are and the gifts with which God has blessed them. Invite individuals or small groups to share in the weekday ministry. A farmer might bring a baby lamb for the children to bottle-feed. A seamstress might make dress-up outfits for the dramatic play center. A musician might bring an instrument one day and teach the children some simple musical concepts. Pay attention to who makes up the congregation and find ways to incorporate them into the weekday ministry. Ask people for their guidance and opinions. If you are doing a project about birds, talk to the person who owns a pet store about the things children should know before buying a pet bird. Learn from the congregation and use their wisdom to benefit the weekday ministry.

Learning From Parents and the Community

Within the larger community, there may be a diversity of cultures within a culture. Learn from the variety so that the weekday ministry can speak the many languages of the children who participate in it. Find out what the family issues are. What is the percentage of single-parent families? blended families? foster families? extended families? Are there any cultural traditions that influence how children are treated or taught in their homes?

Like members of the congregation, parents and people in the community come with unique skills and talents. Invite them to take part in the weekday program in whatever ways they are able to. Seek out specialized knowledge or experience in areas that would interest the children.

Tap into community resources. Take advantage of the specialized resources that are available from the local school, the public library, recreation centers, senior-citizen organizations, service organizations, and local businesses. The community offers resources, information, and support. Learning from the community and the congregation will make education through the weekday ministry even more valuable to everyone involved.

SAMPLE INFANT AND TODDLER CARE DAILY REPORT

Child's Name: _____

Date: _____

Care Provider: _____

Ate:

Slept:

Diapered:

Overall Disposition:

Observations/Questions/Concerns:

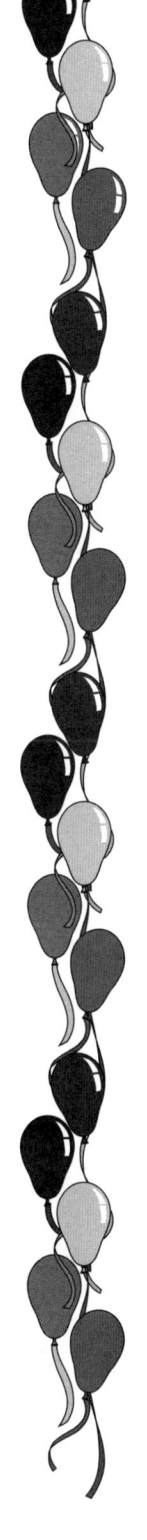

SAMPLE PRESCHOOL DAILY REPORT

Child's Name

Date

Preschool Teacher

Centers child played in

Children child played with

Child's disposition

PRESCHOOL DEVELOPMENTAL CHECKLIST

Student _____

Teacher _____

Date _____

COGNITIVE DEVELOPMENT

Key to Marking System
L   Learning in progress
P   Performs skills presented
Blank   Skill not introduced or evaluated at this time

Colors: ___ Can match 8   ___ Can point to 8   ___ Can name 8

Shapes: <u>Can match</u>   <u>Can name</u>
   Circle
   Square
   Triangle
   Rectangle
   Oval

___ Can name major body parts

Numbers: ___ Can count 0-10   ___ Can answer "Give me 3 items"
         ___ Can match 0-5   ___ Can match 0-10
         ___ Can put in sequence 0-10

___ Can sing ABC's   ___ Can say ABC's   ___ Can match ABC's

Knows the sounds of letters _____

___ Can rhyme words

Child's own name: ___ Can find name   ___ Can match name
                ___ Can write name   ___ Can name letters of name

Picture cards: (Can point to) ___ Vehicles   ___ Clothing
                            ___ Animals   ___ Foods   ___ Household Items

Can classify: ___ Foods ___ Toys   ___ Vehicles
          ___ Pets ___ Clothing

Knows concepts: ___Big/Little   ___Tall/Short   ___Long/Short
               ___Loud/Quiet   ___Hard/Soft   ___Rough/Smooth
               ___Fast/Slow   ___Heavy/Light   ___In front of/Behind
               ___In/Out   ___Top/Bottom

___ Can sequence 4-5 cards in order

___ Can classify by color   ___ Can classify by texture
___ Can classify by size   ___ Can classify by shape

Knows personal data: ___ Name   ___ Address   ___ Birthday

___ Can identify what does not belong

BEHAVIOR RUBRIC

Behavior Skill	Always	Most of Time	Sometimes	Not Enough
Respects Authority 1. Listens to authority 2. Follows directions 3. Accepts responsibility				
Respects Rights of Others 1. Uses appropriate voice and language 2. Listens to speaker 3. Respects opinions of others 4. Respects self 5. Refrains from disturbing others				
Respects Property				
Displays a Concern for Learning 1. Remains on task 2. Allows others to remain on task 3. Responds appropriately to questions				
Displays Appropriate Social Skills 1. Copes (with disagreement, teasing) 2. Displays courtesy and tact 3. Interacts with others appropriately				
Displays Appropriate Character 1. Displays positive character (honest, trustworthy, forgiving, kind) 2. Displays productive character (patient, takes initiative, thorough)				

Comments:

Chapter Twelve
SCHOOL-AGE PROGRAMS

WEEKDAY MINISTRIES

The National Institute on Out-of-School Time reports research showing that for children and youth, organized activities after school are connected with such positive things as better school attendance, improved academic performance, and a reduction in juvenile crime, but that there are approximately 4 million children between the ages of five and twelve who regularly spend time without adult supervision (see "Making the Case: A Fact Sheet on Children and Youth in Out-of-School Time," NIOST, 2003). The need for quality school-age programs exists in just about every community.

School-age programs provide an opportunity for children to meet together for age-appropriate activities in a supervised environment. They also provide relief for parents during long summer days when school is not in session and assurance for parents who must work during the before- and afterschool hours.

The Purpose of the School-Age Program

School-age programs serve many purposes. They can provide an opportunity for children to be tutored in their schoolwork or assisted with their homework. School-age programs provide a safe place for children to go before and after school when no adult would be at home. Some programs offer a basic religious education, continuing the role of the Sunday school into the weekdays. Life skills and decision-making can be taught through school-age programs. Children can learn to prepare snacks, work cooperatively on projects, and even provide services for others in the church or community.

The purpose of a school-age program will shape its content, frequency, and schedule. Determine the content by the need of the children and families in the area. Are children left alone during the afterschool hours? Do neighborhood children go unsupervised during the summer while their parents work? The needs of the community will help to determine whether the church should offer an afterschool program, a summer recreation program, a homework/tutoring program, or a one-afternoon-a-week fellowship/religious-education program.

Once the purpose has been determined, decisions can be made regarding financing and staffing.

Schedule and Activities

Once the need and the purpose are determined, other elements can be planned. The schedule should take into account where the children have been before arriving, the time of day, and how long the children will be at the weekday ministry. Children who have been in school all day will need a snack and activities that will allow them to work off stored-up energy. A summer program can schedule a variety of activities and provide choices for children. A typical schedule will include a snack, conversation time, activities that use large muscles, structured learning, and fun and free-choice times.

Snacks should consist of food that is beneficial to the children and not simply fill them up on sugar or empty calories. Variety is the key. Snacks that children can help prepare offer experiences in food preparation and group cooperation.

Children need time to converse with others. Time to talk, laugh, and joke with one another is important in the social development of school-age children. Talk that involves name-calling or cursing or in any way might injure the ego of another child should not be tolerated.

School-age children need an outlet for energy. Gross motor activities help them work off energy while they develop coordination. Noncompetitive games that allow them to run, jump, and throw and challenge them to develop new skills can serve this purpose. Competitive games can be used as long as they do not result in labeling winners and losers to the extent that some children are humiliated through the experience. Choosing teams can be a painful experience for children who are always the last to be chosen. Teams can be chosen by numbering off or pulling out X's and O's from a hat or other such means. Use methods that do not leave certain children standing alone while no one wants them on their team. Remember, it is an experience of God's accepting love in Jesus Christ that children need to be offered.

Structured learning can be as simple as an introduction to a theme, a Bible-study time, or a time for research and exploration. Structured learning can be done in ways that allow children to move, talk together, and have fun, rather than sitting still while listening to an adult lecture.

Themes

Themes can be fun to work with. Themes allow staff and children to plan activities and projects that revolve around a certain topic for several days or weeks. Activity centers help organize children to offer them a variety of experiences. Possible centers for a school-age program might

What cultural diversities do you find in the community in which the weekday ministry serves?

include: arts and crafts, blocks or construction, drama, music, science exploration, snack preparation, table games, reading center, and a homework center.

Be creative or invite children's involvement in naming activity centers. For example, "Children's World Learning Centers" (see chapter 14 for information about their website) identify centers as the Diner, the Arcade, the University, the Lounge, Center Stage, and the Studio.

Equipment Needs

Equipment needs for school-age programs are similar to early childhood programs with the exception that there will need to be age-appropriate activities for older children. Homework helps might include dictionaries, encyclopedias, adults and older youth to assist, and computers. A computer with a CD-ROM drive is advisable in a program for school-age children. Games for learning, adventure, and exploration can be played on a computer. Pay attention to the goals of the program and the values you want to teach when choosing computer programs. Avoid games that cause children to become aggressive or hyperactive.

Outdoor equipment can provide an opportunity for children to climb, jump, crawl, and swing. Proper supervision at all times is necessary. Rules for school-age children should be posted and reviewed regularly.

Arrival and Dismissal

The arrival and dismissal of school-aged children needs to be worked out according to where they are coming from and where they are to go upon dismissal. Many programs provide an arrival/departure procedures form for parents to fill out. The form simply states how and with whom children will arrive at the center and how and with whom children will depart. If a child lives within walking distance of the school or home and parents agree to let the child walk, that should be stated on the form. No child should ever be released to a person who has not been authorized on the form to pick up the child, unless a parent has made arrangements with the ministry ahead of time.

When children are arriving at the weekday ministry directly from school, check with the school to see if arrangements can be made for the school bus to deliver the children to the center. Determine who is responsible for the children directly before and after the weekday ministry. This may need to be spelled out in the arrival/departure form.

Following a check-in and check-out procedure is a good safety precaution. Regardless of how children arrive, there should be a way for them to check in. It could be signing in on a clipboard or placing a sticker on a chart. As children leave, a similar checkout system can be used. This helps to account for all children as they come and go. For certain types of programs a policy can be made that no one leaves the weekday-ministry program in the middle of a session unless arrangements have been made with a parent. Children who come stay for the entire session. Exceptions are made with the parent face-to-face or over the telephone. Written notes brought in by children are not acceptable forms of communication with parents.

Developmentally Appropriate Programming

When the school-age program involves a wide age group, accommodations will need to be made that provide for developmentally appropriate experiences for everyone. With multiple staff, children can be divided into age groups for certain activities. Remember, however, that much learning takes place as children of various ages work together and help one another. At the same time, a child of six cannot be expected to feel affirmed by trying to put together the same 3-D puzzle that a child of twelve might enjoy. Activity choices must be provided for a wide range of developmental levels.

Age Groupings

The National Network for Child Care (see "Developmentally Appropriate Programming for School-Age Children," by Carole L. Eller and Maureen T. Mulroy, www.nncc.org/SACC/dev.approp.sac.html) has identified three age groups among elementary-school–age children:
- Young School-Age Child: Children in K-2
- Middle School-Age Child: Children in grades 3-4
- Older School-Age Child: Children in grades 5-6

Some age-appropriate activities for each age group might include the following (some of which also come from the NNCC study cited above).

Young School-Age Children

Gross Motor Development—Children this age enjoy running, jumping, throwing, and catching. Games like "Mother May I?" and "Redlight/Greenlight" and tag are also fun.

Fine Motor Development—Eye-hand coordination practice, such as cutting, gluing, drawing, painting, puzzles, writing, and small manipulatives, is important for this age group.

Social Skills—Home center, dolls and puppets, blocks, roads, trains, cars, doll house, dress-up, and roleplaying are all appropriate for young school-age children.

Cognitive Skills—Matching, sorting, arranging, books, letter games, number games, music, and perception activities help this age group develop important cognitive skills.

Spiritual Development—Children this age can understand that God loves us and we can love God, that God made us, that we know God's love through Jesus Christ, that we celebrate Jesus' birth at Christmas, that God made all things, that all things can become new, and that we can love one another. This is a good age to introduce Bible stories.

Middle School-Age Children

Gross Motor Development—Middle school-age children are ready to develop the physical skills of more organized team sports and to learn the rules of the games. Be sure to let everyone play and give all children the chance to succeed.

Fine Motor Development—These children enjoy using a variety of materials and styles for arts and crafts, using real tools and utensils, and delving into touch, taste, sight, smell, and sound.

Social Skills—The community at large is of interest to them—how things work, what the workers do, what they might do when they grow up, making and using maps, and uncovering "treasures" or finding things that are hidden.

Cognitive Skills—Children enjoy using the skills they have in new and creative ways. They like problem-solving, construction, and riddles.

Spiritual Development—Middle school-age children can become more familiar with the Bible, how it is put together, and the difference between the Old and New Testaments. They can read better than younger school-age children. They enjoy dramatizing what they read, illustrating it, and making the Bible stories come alive. Prayer can be more creative than memorizing words, and music is fun for them.

Older School-Age Children

Gross Motor Development—These children have much more control of the movement of their bodies and can engage in more structured activities. They are ready to learn the detailed rules of team sports.

Fine Motor Development—Older children have much more control of their fine motor skills than younger ones do. They enjoy making models, building, woodworking, and arts and crafts that require creativity and decision-making.

Social Skills—Older children are interested in the world outside the neighborhood. They want to learn about people in other places, including their culture, food, rituals, language, and dress. Social-service activities are appropriate for this age group. Older children value a "best friend" and find security in a small circle of close friends.

Cognitive Skills—These children enjoy problem-solving and exploring a variety of possible answers. They are beginning to form their own opinions and like to compare one person's opinion with another person's opinion. They like having research materials available to explore the world and seek answers to their questions.

Spiritual Development—These children can read well and have the ability to research questions. They will enjoy using a concordance and other Bible helps. They are able to discuss a passage of Scripture more easily and share opinions. Encouragement in prayer and in keeping a personal journal is helpful to them.

Remember that developmentally appropriate practice takes into consideration not only a child's age but also a child's culture, physical and mental development, and experience. Do not expect all children in kindergarten to second grade, for instance, to fall into the descriptions above. Use the descriptions as a general guideline. Provide options for children to choose from. The children themselves can best determine which activities are most appropriate for them.

Afterschool programs could also be designed for children who are in middle school and junior high. Consider the needs of the community and your available resources when determining the ages to be served.

Centers

Centers can be useful in providing experiences for different age groups. While older children construct a papier-mâché landscape in one center, younger children can be using paper, glue, and stickers to make signs that represent products that grow in the different areas of the landscape. While younger children play at the water table, older children can be challenged to construct a water wheel that will actually work in the science center. Younger children might enjoy a "riddle of the day," while older children can wrestle with a daily brainteaser.

How children are divided into activities should largely be the choice of the individual child. Children usually choose activities that reflect their developmental level. One child may be well developed in physical coordination but will need the simplest project to feel affirmed when it comes to art.

Some children are quick to memorize a Bible verse, while other children find memorization extremely frustrating. They might be better off acting out a passage of Scripture or looking up unknown words that are used in the verse. Use your imagination and pay attention to the leading of the children as you plan a school-age program.

A school-age program can be fun for everyone. It can provide assurance for parents, structure and supervision for children, and a service to the community.

Chapter Thirteen
Sustaining a Quality Program

Sustaining a quality weekday ministry requires attention in the following areas: (1) regular evaluations of the program; (2) staff assessment; (3) a supportive relationship between the church and the weekday ministry; (4) a good rapport between the weekday ministry and the larger community; (5) continuous awareness of the needs in the community and the needs which the weekday ministry addresses.

Program Evaluations

The Board of Directors

Regular evaluation of the weekday ministry is the responsibility of the board of directors or the group within the church that has administrative responsibility for the weekday ministry. Although some form of evaluation will take place at each meeting, an annual meeting solely for the purpose of evaluation is most effective. This could be done in one full day or as a retreat. Meeting in the space provided for the weekday ministry makes identifying space and equipment needs much easier. This formal evaluation is best done at a time before budget proposals need to be in and when repairs and staff changes are most easily made. For weekday ministries that are scheduled around the school year, summer is an appropriate time for in-depth evaluations. A summer evaluation allows time for making any necessary changes. For weekday ministries that are year-round, fall can be a good time for evaluation, since this is usually when new budgets are being prepared, new officers are being elected, and churches are meeting for charge conference. An evaluation of the weekday ministry should take place before charge conference so that the chairperson will have a complete report about the past year and plans for the coming years to share with the church.

Input for Program Evaluation

In order for a program evaluation to be most effective, the board of directors should seek input from everyone involved. That would include input from program staff, parents, church staff, the congregation, and the larger community. A simple form is best. No one likes to get bogged down with answering a lot of detailed questions. Three or four direct questions will call forth the information you are looking for: "What needs is the weekday ministry meeting? How might these needs be better met? State any concerns you have regarding the weekday ministry." These few questions will allow the church council, church staff, and individuals from the congregation to share affirmations and concerns about the weekday ministry.

An evaluation form for parents could be more detailed. Parental evaluations could be given to the parents at parent-teacher conference time to be sent back, or mailed to parents with a monthly newsletter. The easier it is for parents to receive and return them, the more evaluations will be completed.

If the weekday ministry goes through the process of accreditation by a nationally recognized organization such as the National Association for the Education of Young Children, a lengthy program evaluation will be part of the process. Use this opportunity and learn from it. Take from it things you find most helpful and continue to benefit from them as the program continues.

Key Questions

Program evaluation helps to determine the strength of the weekday ministry and areas where improvement is needed. Key questions to consider might include:

- Is the curriculum developmentally appropriate?
- Is the weekday ministry meeting an existing need?
- What could be done to make the space a safer place for children?
- Are the meals and snacks nutritionally beneficial to the children?
- What are the concerns of the staff?
- What are the concerns of the parents?
- What are the concerns of the church?
- What are the concerns of the board of directors?
- Does the budget meet programming needs?
- Does the budget meet staff needs?
- Are the fundraising activities both effective and appropriate for a church-based ministry?
- Are program goals being met?
- Are tuition and fees comparable to those of similar programs in the area?
- Are licensing requirements being met?
- Is the program accredited through a national organization?
- Should the program become accredited?
- Are the program space and equipment kept in sanitary conditions?
- Are the toys and equipment in good repair?
- Are the walls, floors, and fixtures in good repair?

- Is the number of staff people right for achieving the desired quality for the program?
- Are more staff needed?
- Are fewer staff needed?
- Are there issues among the staff that need to be addressed?
- Are there issues related to parents that need to be addressed?
- Are there issues related to the church that need to be addressed?
- Are there issues related to the board of directors that need to be addressed?
- Are there issues related to the community that need to be addressed?
- Is the program being effectively marketed?

Staff Assessments

The purpose of staff assessments is to help staff fulfill their job descriptions in ways that help to meet the program goals. As a program changes, staff roles may also change. Assessments help to point out where changes in staff or staff job descriptions need to be made. Staff assessment is a tool for encouraging growth and affirming the God-given gifts of each staff member. It should be conducted in ways that are helpful to the staff rather than demoralizing.

Staff assessments should be done regularly, at least annually. That will avoid the threat that comes when assessments are conducted only when a problem arises. One of the benefits of regular staff assessment is that it often helps to address issues before they become a major problem.

The staff assessment can be conducted in a number of ways. The most helpful assessments do not depend solely on one source of information.

What other questions might be important in sustaining a quality weekday ministry?

Self-Assessment

The self-assessment can be one of the most beneficial sources of information pertaining to staff effectiveness. Self-assessment offers individual staff members a chance to reflect on their own performance. Statement-based forms can be used as tools for self-reflection. The statements can be general enough to be used for a variety of staff roles. Some possible statements are as follows:
- I feel good about my job when ...
- I feel inadequate when ...
- This year I have found ... most helpful in equipping me for my job.
- This year has been most frustrating when it comes to ...
- One thing I would like to do better in my job is ...
- An issue that is of concern for me is ...
- One thing that needs to be celebrated about this year is ...
- One thing I would like to learn/practice during the next year is ...

A space for staff members to write down the continuing education credit they have earned this year is also helpful.

Peer/Supervisor's Assessment

Sometimes it takes someone other than oneself to be able to identify job strengths and point out areas that need to be strengthened. An assessment done by one member of the staff for the sake of another member of the staff or one done by the supervisor can be helpful. If a staff is experiencing a lot of friction between people, a peer assessment may feel threatening, if not unfair. However, if that kind of friction exists, assessment time is the perfect opportunity to address the issues involved, with the goal of making staff relationships more positive.

A peer or supervisor's assessment can also be guided by a series of statements:

- The staff person is most effective at . . .
- The staff person could be more effective in the area of . . .
- One thing I have appreciated about this staff person this year is . . .
- One thing I would have liked this staff person to do differently this year is . . .
- This staff person might benefit from a continuing education event in the area of . . .

Design statements to be positive, while not ignoring areas that need work. A balance of appreciation and direction is the key to an effective staff evaluation.

Video Assessment

Another approach that is helpful for staff is to videotape the staff at work. Tape a day, or segments of a few days, and have the staff sit down together to view themselves with a critical but caring eye. Most people will be most critical about themselves, especially on video. Once everyone gets over commenting about how much weight they need to lose, or how their hair looked a mess, run the tape a small portion at a time. When someone notices something that might have been handled more effectively, or something that was handled well, pause the tape for discussion. For a staff person who is brand-new, or may be presenting particular concerns, a viewing of the tape with only the staff person and supervisor present may be most helpful.

Relationship Between the Church and Weekday Ministry

The relationship between the church and the weekday ministry can determine the longevity of the program. Since the weekday program is a ministry of the church, the church has the power to discontinue the weekday ministry if it so chooses. Programs that are not sponsored by the church but use space provided by the church run the risk of the church deciding to use the space for another purpose or simply choosing not to "rent" the space any longer. Full support from the church is a necessary element for the long-term survival of a weekday ministry.

Keep the Weekday Ministry Visible

Church support requires that the people who make up the church have a clear understanding of the weekday ministry and feel a certain ownership of it. This is accomplished through frequent and ongoing communication with the congregation. Share not only the needs of the weekday ministry but also the successes, the joy of working with the children, and the difference the program is making in families. Use the weekly bulletin, the church newsletter, a bulletin board, church meetings, and fellowship times to share an enthusiasm for what is happening in the church through the weekday ministry.

Involve the Congregation

Ask for advice from members of the congregation. Being asked makes people feel important. The church is filled with teachers, both active and retired, social workers, parents and grandparents, and children who can be resources for the life of a weekday ministry. Visit Sunday school classes, small groups in the church, and both formal and informal gatherings so that the weekday ministry is as visible as possible. Invite groups to come visit during the weekday-ministry hours or to share their talents and interests in some way with the children or families who participate in the program. For example, have a class adopt a grandparent or invite members to read stories. The more people in the congregation who are used some way in the life of the weekday ministry, the better the church will understand the mission of the program and its impact on the lives of people.

Handle Problems Head-on

When problems arise with a group or individual in the church, the problem should be addressed in a timely manner with love and diplomacy. For example, the kitchen committee does not like having to give up counter space for the labeled cups used by the daycare. No one has talked to you directly, but a couple of people have mentioned that "the ladies are upset." You could ignore it and hope the problem goes away. You could make a snide remark about the selfishness of some people in the church at the next church council meeting. Neither of these options would be productive for the longevity of the weekday ministry.

Go directly to the person on the kitchen committee who has been designated as the liaison to the weekday ministry. If there is no such person, go to the committee chair. Let him or her know that you have heard these things said and that you are concerned that there might be a problem. Be willing to work things out. It may be as simple as placing all the daycare cups on one large tray so that it is easy to move them aside, or it could open up a new opportunity to dialogue with the kitchen committee. Someone on the committee may have a wonderful solution if they are given a chance to be heard.

Upkeep of Equipment and Facilities

The longevity of a program requires continuous upkeep of equipment and facilities. Neglect results in costly replacement of items that could have been salvaged if cared for properly. When a crack starts, get it filled. When a screw falls out, replace it immediately. If it's sharp, sand it down. If it has splinters, sand and seal it. If an accident occurs in the same situation more than once, change the situation. Work with the board of trustees, the board of directors, and church custodian to stay on top of equipment and facility needs. Many churches have a memorial committee that may be able to direct memorial gifts toward equipment that would benefit the weekday ministry. The facility is the first thing people will observe when arriving at the weekday-ministry site. Allow the facility and equipment to speak a message of safety, fun, and love.

Good Rapport With the Community

Just as the relationship between the weekday ministry and church is important for the longevity of a program, so is the relationship with the larger community. The size of that community depends on the mission of the program. It could be the neighborhood, the town, certain sections within a city, or an entire city. The community is the area to which the ministry of the weekday program is extended.

As you keep the weekday ministry visible to the people in the church, it must also be visible to the larger community. Newspaper articles about activities, flyers in the community, advertisements in local publications, and other media exposure all help to keep the community informed about the ministry. If a group of children are taking Valentine's Day plates to residents at a local long-term-care center, let a local news organization know. News agencies are often looking for human-interest stories that relate to the local community and especially to children.

Listen to the needs of the community. Stay up-to-date on statistics that relate to the population the weekday ministry serves. Be alert to needs that are not being met to see if there would be any way to address one or more of them through the weekday ministry.

Involve community leaders any way you can in the weekday ministry. Invite the mayor, the fire chief, the health nurse, the dentist, and the man who raises hedgehogs to share their knowledge, work, or hobbies with the children. Plan field trips within the community. Through field trips children are educated about the community and the community is educated about the weekday ministry.

Whether you are working with people in the church or people in the larger community, express appreciation to them through friendly messages or thank-you cards. Let them know that they have made an impact on the children in the program. Mention them by name in the church newsletter, the weekday-ministry newsletter, or the local newspaper. Involve the children in the program in expressing gratitude; they can make thank-you drawings, create cards, or send small gifts that all of them helped to make.

Continuous Assessment of Needs and Program Goals

As time passes, communities change and needs change. The longer a weekday ministry continues, the more important it becomes to reassess the needs of the community and the goals of the program. Review the mission statement. Is the mission of the weekday ministry still valid? Do the program goals meet the needs of the participants?

In the 1980's many churches started Mother's-Day-Out programs. As time has passed, more and more mothers have entered the full-time work force. Now many Mother's-Day-Out programs are being replaced by daycare programs or afterschool programs because these better fit the needs of community families. As needs change, the mission and goals for ministry change.

Conclusion

Regular program evaluations will help keep you in touch with the needs of the community and the validity of the ministry being offered. Open communication with the congregation and the larger community will provide valuable information regarding needs and concerns and how the weekday ministry might continue over time.

As in every step of dreaming, planning, and implementing a weekday ministry, prayer and discernment are vital for the ongoing life of a program and those who provide for it. You are a minister, a servant leader. Let the love of Jesus Christ be your focus, and the Spirit of God your source of energy.

Chapter Fourteen

Resources for a Weekday Ministry

WEEKDAY MINISTRIES

Resources for weekday ministries are everywhere. You will find them in your community, in your church, on your computer, in books and magazines, and any place you are willing to open your eyes and see them. Listed in the chapter are only a few of the resources that are available to you.

Resources in the Church

Church resources include both the resources that are available in your local church as well as district, conference, and general church resources.

Local Church Resources

Your local church membership is a vast sea of knowledge, skills, experiences, interests, hobbies, and personalities. The church officers often receive information from the annual conference about events or publications that could be a helpful resource for the weekday ministry. Let them know that you are interested in anything that comes their way. The church staff also has access to many resources that could be beneficial.

District and Conference Resources

District and annual conference leaders can be a great aid in discovering resources. Workshops, seminars, speakers, and other conference events may be planned that could be used as part of staff training. Conference agencies such as colleges, urban and rural ministries, health ministries, and ministries to youth and their families all have experts in these areas. Tap these resources. Involve the annual conference in whatever way you can. There may be a professor at a nearby United Methodist college who would be willing to spend time with the weekday-ministry staff for a training event. The director of an urban-ministries program or a health-ministries

List names of agencies and people in your district and annual conference who might be a resource to the weekday ministry.

agency might help identify the needs and issues that families in your community are dealing with. The conference chancellor can be helpful with legal questions and advice.

General Church Resources

The general church boards and agencies can provide resources beyond your local community. Listed below is contact information for some of the agencies.

General Board of Church and Society, 100 Maryland Avenue NE, Washington, DC 20002 (www.umc-gbcs.org). Sponsors a child-advocacy network to address the needs of children.

General Board of Discipleship, PO Box 340003, Nashville, TN 37203 (www.gbod.org/children). Provides resources, events, and training, including Focus (an event for children's leaders) and resources to support the United Methodist Fund for Children's Mission.

General Board of Global Ministries, 475 Riverside Drive, New York, NY 10115 (gbgm-umc.org). Provides information on mission education.

General Council on Finance and Administration, 1200 Davis Street, Evanston, IL 60201 (www.gcfa.org). Can provide information related to tax exemption, incorporation, and other legal and financial issues.

Cokesbury (www.cokesbury.com). A division of the United Methodist Publishing House that provides curriculum resources.

Resources in the Community

Community resources are as numerous as you are willing to imagine. Some possibilities are
- Local schools
- Educators
- Musicians
- Youth talent
- Professionals in every area
- Actors
- Service people
- Colleges and universities
- Parents
- Extended family members
- Plants, factories, farms, orchards, and other businesses
- Law-enforcement agencies
- Hospitals
- Libraries
- Animal specialists
- Accountants and tax experts
- Chambers of commerce
- Local service organizations

Books

New books are being published every day. Check with a local college or university to find out what books are on the reading list for classes that apply to the mission of the weekday ministry. What are they reading in education classes, children's literature, child development? A few books that might be helpful are listed here. NAEYC and SchoolAge Notes are particularly well-respected publishers.

Before and After School Programs: A Start-Up and Administration Manual, by Mary McDonald Richard (School-Age Notes, 1991).

Developmentally Appropriate Practice in Early Childhood Programs, revised edition, edited by Sue Bredekamp and Carol Copple (National Association for the Education of Young Children, 1997).

Eager to Learn: Educating Our Preschoolers, edited by Barbara T. Bowman, M. Suzanne Donovan, and M. Susan Burns (National Academy Press, 2001).

Early Childhood Education Today, eighth edition, by George S. Morrison (Prentice-Hall, 2000).

Early Childhood Environment Rating Scale, revised edition, by Thelma Harms, Richard M. Clifford, and Debby Cryer (Teachers College Press, 1998).

The First Three Years: A Guide for Ministry With Infants, Toddlers, and Two-Year-Olds, revised and updated, edited by Mary Alice Gran (Discipleship Resources, 2001).

Helping Churches Mind the Children: A Guide for Church-Housed Child Care Programs, revised edition, by the National Council of Churches of Christ in the United States of America (All Union Press, 1987). Available through the Ecumenical Child Care Network.

Safe Sanctuaries: Reducing the Risk of Child Abuse in the Church, by Joy Thornburg Melton (Discipleship Resources, 1998).

Teaching Young Children: A Guide for Teachers and Leaders, by Mary-Jane Pierce Norton (Discipleship Resources, 1997).

Working With Young Children, by Judy Herr (Goodheart-Wilcox Company, 1998).

Other Print Resources

Many organizations print resources for childcare, early childhood education, and school-age activities. Look to your state licensing agency and also to accreditation agencies. Magazines such as *Scholastic Early Childhood Today* and *Mailbox* offer ideas and articles about related issues. Professional journals like *Young Children* can keep you informed on issues, research, and available resources in the area of early childhood education. School-Age Notes is a national resource organization on school-age care. Talk to directors of similar programs to find out what print resources they have found helpful.

List names of people and organizations in your community who might be a resource to the weekday ministry.

Organizations

Afterschool Alliance
PO Box 65166
Washington, DC 20035
202-296-9378
www.afterschoolalliance.org

Child Care Aware
(a program of the National Association of Child Care Resource and
Referral Agencies)
1319 F. Street, NW
Suite 500
Washington, DC 20004
800-424-2246
www.childcareaware.org
(Has a link for finding the resource and referral agency in your area.)

Ecumenical Child Care Network
PO Box 803586
Chicago, IL 60680
312-829-6284 or 800-694-5443
eccn@aol.com
www.eccn.org
Provides accreditation for childcare programs in church-related settings
compatible with NAEYC accreditation.

Harvard Family Research Project
Harvard Graduate School of Education
3 Garden Street
Cambridge, MA 02138
617-495-9108
gseweb.harvard.edu/~hfrp

National Academy of Early Childhood Programs
National Association for the Education of Young Children
1509 16th Street, NW
Washington, DC 20036
800-424-2460, ext. 11360
academy@naeyc.org
www.naeyc.org

National Association of Child Care Resource and Referral Agencies
(NACCRRA)
1319 F. Street, NW
Suite 500
Washington, DC 20004
202-393-5501
www.naccrra.org

The National School-Age Care Alliance
1137 Washington Street
Boston, MA 02124
617-298-5012
staff@nsaca.org
www.nsaca.org

School-Age Notes
PO Box 40205
Nashville, TN 37204
615-279-0700 or 800-410-8780
www.schoolagenotes.com

List resources you see in your local church. Be as specific as possible.

Other Internet Resources

Early Childhood Resources

EarlyChildhood.com (www.earlychildhood.com): A source of information for all who share an interest in improving the education and general life experience of young children.

Early Childhood Education Online (www.ume.maine.edu/ECEOL-L/): Offers support and opportunities for the exchange of information to all educators and others who want children to have quality learning experiences.

ERIC (ericeece.org): Clearinghouse on elementary and early childhood education. From the University of Illinois at Urbana–Champaign. This site includes lots of links.

National Association for the Education of Young Children (www.naeyc.org): *Young Children* magazine, public-policy updates, finding accredited early childhood/childcare programs, and guidelines on developmentally appropriate practices.

Phi Delta Kappa (www.pdkintl.org): An international organization for professional educators. It promotes quality education, with particular emphasis on publicly supported education, as essential to nurturing and sustaining a democratic way of life. The site includes the *Kappan* magazine.

Infant and Toddler Resources

I Am Your Child (www.iamyourchild.org): A national public-awareness and engagement foundation seeking to make early childhood development a top priority for our nation. I Am Your Child has educated millions of parents and professionals about breakthrough new discoveries in the process of brain development and about other development issues.

Parents as Teachers (www.patnc.org): A program designed to provide all parents of children, from before birth to age five, the information and support they need to give their children the best possible start in life. Offers links related to kids' needs, family education, kids' health, and more.

Zero to Three (www.zerotothree.org): Contains weekly parenting tips and news items related to infants, toddlers, and families.

School-Age Resources

Afterschool.gov (www.afterschool.gov): A site focused on federal resources related to the time children spend out of school. Information is provided on subjects from running a program to planning activities to keeping current on issues.

Children's World (www.childrensworld.com). Children's World Learning Centers offer quality care for children of all ages. Browsing their site may be helpful as you develop your own center.

National Institute on Out-of-School Time (www.niost.org). Their fact sheet "Making the Case," along with other research and information about children's out-of-school time, can be downloaded in PDF form from their Publications page.

National School-Age Care Alliance (www.nsaca.org): A network for after-school professionals, full of information and links to more information.

School-Age Notes (www.schoolagenotes.com): A catalog of resources for school-age programs and those who work with school-age children.

Programs and Ideas

About Daycare/Preschool (www.daycare.about.com): Provides lots of information for daycare providers and preschool teachers.

Ask the Preschool Teacher (www.askthepreschoolteacher.com): Ask questions, receive news, and find lots of printables for preschool teachers.

Craftsnhobbies (www.craftsnhobbies.com): Free craft instructions for all ages. Includes lots of ideas and theme-related crafts.

Idea Box (www.theideabox.com): Resources for early childhood education and activities, including ideas and message boards.

The Perpetual Preschool (www.perpetualpreschool.com): This site was built to celebrate the creativity and dedication of all those who contribute to the perpetual education of young children. It includes ideas for different kinds of play and other activities.

Preschool by Stormie (www.preschoolbystormie.com): This website is designed to aid prekindergarten teachers. It is not necessarily for an expert in early childhood education; the goal is to offer teachers a place to share ideas used in the classroom.

Special Needs

Childswork/Childsplay (www.childswork.com): Offers information and resources on children's social and emotional needs.

Council for Exceptional Children (www.cec.sped.org): Publishes extremely up-to-date news regarding education-related legislation and contains links to other sites.

IDEA Practices (www.ideapractices.org): This site seeks to answer questions about the Individuals with Disabilities Education Act, let educators know about ideas that work, and offer support to efforts to help all children learn and develop.

Parent Education

Family Education (www.familyeducation.com): This site offers resources and information on the counseling, education, resources, and training needed to promote a positive and nurturing environment for children.

The National Parenting Center (www.tnpc.com): Provides parents with guidance from renowned authorities on child-rearing.

The Natural Child Project (www.naturalchild.com/home/): Dedicated to teaching parents and others about the importance of early childhood and to promoting the practice of treating children with dignity and respect.

National Parent Information Network (www.npin.org): Identifies specific Internet resources for parents and those who work with them.

Parenthood.com (www.parenthood.com): Articles and product information for parents. Includes a calendar of events for each state.

Parents Planet (www.parents-planet.com): A web guide for parents.

Parent Soup (www.parentsoup.com): Offers resources and features on a wide array of educational topics.

Teaching Resources and Supplies

ABC School Supply Online (www.abcschoolsupply.com).

Classroom Direct (www.classroomdirect.com): A superstore for discount educational supplies.

Constructive Playthings (www.cptoys.com/school/default.asp).

EarlyChildhood.com (www.earlychildhood.com): This site also sells supplies and equipment through its Discount School Supply page.

eNASCO On-Line Catalogs (www.enasco.com/prod/Home): NASCO was started in 1941 by an educator trying to develop teaching aids for his classroom. NASCO still seeks to offer products that appropriately meet the needs of real classrooms.

Kaplan (www.kaplanco.com).

Lakeshore Learning Materials (www.lakeshorelearning.com).

PlayKids (www.playkids.com): Indoor and outdoor equipment and toys.

Train a Brain (www.trainabrain.com).

Unlimited Resources

New resources are always being developed. One resource may lead to another. You will never exhaust all resources as long as you continue to pay attention to what is available and tap into existing resources.

**Here is a place for your
personal Internet log.**